THE VALUE SALE

THE
VALUE
SALE

How to Prove ROI and Win More Deals

IAN CAMPBELL

LIONCREST
PUBLISHING

THE VALUE SALE
How to Prove ROI and Win More Deals

FIRST EDITION

ISBN 978-1-5445-4332-1 *Hardcover*
      978-1-5445-4330-7 *Paperback*
      978-1-5445-4331-4 *Ebook*
      978-1-5445-4333-8 *Audiobook*

CONTENTS

THE VALUE SALE

INTRODUCTION

RAISING ALLIGATORS IN THE BATHTUB

What if I told you that you could make great money by buying and raising baby alligators in your bathtub? Would you do it? What if it's the bathtub in the only bathroom in your house, and you'd have to use the bathroom at the gas station down the street for the next year or so?

Well, your first response would probably be a resounding "No!" But, after a moment's consideration, you might follow it up with "How much money could I make?" What if I said you could make $5 million a year? Would you be willing to raise baby alligators in your bathtub for $5 million a year? Probably so.

Even though it's a crazy suggestion, there is a value point above which raising baby alligators in your bathtub becomes a good idea. There's also a number above which your spouse will think you're a genius for signing on the dotted line to raise baby alligators even if they have to use the bathroom down the street for the next year.

Bear in mind, I've shared very few details about the product itself. I told you nothing about the features of baby alligators, how cute they can be, or how they'll be better at protecting the house than a dog. But it doesn't matter as much because of the value I've attached to it. The minute a salesperson proves value, any deal becomes a whole lot easier, even before they've mentioned all of the features of the product.

If you can make a compelling case for the value that a product or service will deliver, and if that value is enough, then people are going to buy in. *Value always drives the deal!* It's really as simple as that, but what happens in most sales meetings? When the salesperson doesn't know what to do, they lead by promoting the features of the product rather than the benefits. They tell the client what the product *does* rather than how the product delivers value for them.

Let's suppose you're selling supply chain management software. You could talk to the client all day long about the various features that the software offers, but leading with the benefits will *always* make a more compelling case for the sale. Which of the following is more likely to convince a prospective customer to buy? The first leads with features, the second with value.

1. "This software provides order and billing management, logistics and transportation tools, and warehouse and inventory management. There are supplier collaboration tools as well, and a fully configurable interface."
2. "This software will increase the productivity of your employees by 15 percent. It will reduce the cost of inventory by 20 percent per year and make it a lot cheaper to manufacture new products because you will be able to manage your supply chain better."

The first pitch focuses on the software's features and leaves it up to the prospect to figure out what benefits those features will deliver. The second leads with value, telling the prospect what the benefits of investing in this product will be. The features can then be tied to those benefits. That's *always* the more compelling case.

Above all, you need to prove to a prospect that the purchase will provide them with positive return on investment (ROI)—they're going to get back more in value than they spend on your solution. If you can do that, you'll make the decision a lot easier for them.

Think about it. If I'm trying to sell you a car, I can tell you, "It's got four tires made of synthetic rubber and steel cord belt plies. It's got four seats covered in nylon upholstery. The body is made of plastic painted lime green, and it's got six windows." Or I can tell you, "This car gets great gas mileage (up to forty miles per gallon on the highway), so you can get where you want to go more efficiently without breaking the bank. It comes with all-weather tires, so you can use it all year long, which means you'll never be stranded. You've been taking Uber to work, and you're tired of it. Well, now you have safe and reliable transportation to get there quicker and cheaper."

Which one is going to make the more compelling case? Clearly the latter. In my experience, leading with benefits is always more effective than leading with features. Tell the customer what value they're going to get from the product or service, convince them of a positive ROI, and you will make a far more compelling case for closing the deal.

And you won't need to challenge the customer or strongarm

them through your sales funnel. If you make a compelling case for the value of the product, then you don't have to back them into the corner and say, "Buy the car today. Why aren't you buying this car today? What will it take to get you to buy the car? How can I convince you to buy the car?"

In fact, I can't say this strongly enough. The idea of challenging, even *bullying*, customers to force them through each stage of your sales funnel may be a popular approach these days, but I think it's *wholly unnecessary*, and even potentially detrimental. All you need to do is talk about the benefits the customer will receive.

The fact is once you prove value, you won't have to *push* the customer through the sale. Value will *pull* them through the funnel. In fact, if you prove value and show them a strong value proposition, the customer will drive the sale themselves. You will be more like a consultant showing them a golden path. Think about it. If I told you that you could make $5 million a year raising alligators, you would be frantically trying to figure out where to order alligators. I wouldn't have to push you into it. The value would be so clear that you would race ahead with no delay.

Proving value is how you close more deals and win more customers every time, *regardless of what you're selling*, whether it's cars, supply chain management software, or alligators!

MAKE THE CONNECTION TO VALUE

When you lead with features, then you rely on the customer to make the connection between your product and their particular needs. In doing so, you're extending the deal time as the customer tries to internalize how your product is going to help them, and the longer you extend the deal time, the more likely you are to lose the deal.

If you don't make a compelling case for the value your product delivers, if you rely on the customer being pre-educated about the value, then they're likely to undervalue what you can do for them. And when that happens, they're going to start asking for discounts.

When *you* make the case, when *you* lead with benefits, then you also justify the cost.

Let's suppose you're trying to sell customers on using the bus to get to work every day rather than driving their own vehicles. You do some research and determine that the average person who drives into the city with their own vehicle has to pay for gas, tolls, parking, and the upkeep on the vehicle. As public transportation becomes more convenient, the financial value of buying a bus pass over driving a personal vehicle becomes a lot clearer.

For $50 a month, they can ride the bus to work without worrying about filling the gas tank, paying for parking, paying tolls, or keeping the car in good shape. Not only is it a lot more convenient, but they are going to save a lot of money over the course of a year. The positive return on their investment is clear! But *you* have to make the case. Show them the value. If you simply explain how the bus pass works and describe its features, then you rely on the customer to calculate the value of buying it. That's when customers say things like "I think a bus pass is worth about $15 a month, not $50. Could I get a discount?"

In my decades of experience, this is a mistake I have seen salespeople make all too often. They lead with features and hope the customer will make the connection to the value themselves. It's an approach that just doesn't work often enough.

At the same time, we've also got so-called experts telling sales reps to "challenge the customer," so not only do they lead with features, but they push prospects aggressively in an attempt to close deals. This approach also isn't effective enough to make it worthwhile.

Do you want to be more effective at sales? Then approach every deal as a consultative partnership, and make a compelling case for the value the customer will get. Most people look at value as ROI. "What's the return for the money I'm going to spend on this product?" We'll talk more in depth about communicating a positive ROI later on, but keep this in mind. You should always lead with benefits and communicate a positive ROI based on those benefits!

That's how you close more deals, make happier customers, and avoid discounts. And this doesn't just apply to sales. Marketing needs to lead with benefits as well, communicating value through all of their marketing materials in order to make it far easier for customers to move through the funnel.

That's it. That's the "big secret" to winning more people over. Stop leading with a "features list," and forget about "challenging" people to move to the next step in the pipeline. Lead with value, make a compelling case for the benefits, *and they will drive themselves through the pipeline!*

FROM PROSPECTS TO CHAMPIONS

So, about now, you might be thinking, *Lead with benefits. You make it sound so simple. But how do I figure out the different kinds of benefits my product can deliver to a prospect? How do I insert value into my message? Which benefits are most compelling? How do I calculate the cost and benefits so I can deliver a credible business base about the return on investment? And how do I help a prospect champion the product internally so they can get the budget for it?*

These are all fair questions, and I'm going to answer each of them in this book. And when you can answer these questions, you don't have to worry about beating someone down to get them to move forward.

If you're selling B2B, then the person you're pitching to usually has to turn around and convince someone else in the company to pay for it. That means you're facing a two-step hurdle: sell to the decision-maker, then help them sell to the person who holds the purse strings. Chances are, you've had deals stall or just disappear after you made what felt like a successful pitch, and you never really found out why.

Usually, it's because there were competing projects in the company vying for the same money that you didn't know about. It's likely that the deal didn't die out; it just didn't beat out the other projects. And in those instances, all of the features in the world, and the most aggressive approach, isn't going to help you.

You know what *will* help you? Making a compelling case about the value of the product that the prospect can use internally. That gives you the ability to win, *even when you're not there!* When a champion can make a rational business case about the value of your product, that's almost always more effective than just passionately pleading or aggressively begging for your product to win the budget.

Look, I've been doing this for a very long time. Over the last two decades, I've worked with hundreds of companies, studied hundreds more, and analyzed the results, taking a hard look at what makes sales effective. I've published over a thousand ROI case studies, and the pattern is very clear. When sales reps lead with value and make a compelling business case about the benefits of their product, they close far more deals and create far more champions.

In the upcoming chapters, I'm going to show you exactly how to make this approach work for you. You will be able to turn right around and implement it, delivering a compelling case about the return on investment of purchasing your product. In fact, I'll be bold enough to say that this is probably the only practical book on sales that you can use the day you finish reading it. I'll provide plenty of examples of how you build an effective and credible business case so that even if there's a two-step sales process, you can give your prospect what they need to champion your product to a financial decision-maker.

Forget challenging customers. Forget about bullying your customers until you wear them down and get them to buy. Forget creating a features list. By the end of this book, you will know everything you need to know to create a consultative relationship with prospects that works *far more often* than any other sales approach on the market!

CHAPTER ONE

VALUE IN THE SALES FUNNEL

Where does "value" fit into your sales funnel? What step is it in the process of turning a prospect into a loyal customer? Think about it for a minute. Where would you introduce value into the conversation? Maybe you should discuss it when you're qualifying a prospect. Or maybe it's better to wait until you give your final proposal. It's an important consideration. If you're going to present a prospect with the value of your product, you have to work it into the funnel *somewhere*, don't you?

Well, actually, I don't believe it fits into *any* specific place in your sales funnel because value is not a stage or a step in the process. Instead, it runs parallel to your sales funnel, and you weave the message into each and every stage along the way. You don't get to the end of your funnel and say, "Okay, now I need to build a compelling business case." If you haven't already done so at every stage before that, then you've missed out on the opportunity to establish credibility about the benefits of your product.

This is a mistake that many salespeople make. You can't simply insert a conversation on value into a single point in the sales funnel because there's no single point in the funnel where ROI exists—and these two things are inextricably linked. Rather, ROI and value must run alongside the entire funnel.

A PARALLEL CONVERSATION

Every sales rep has learned some kind of sales funnel. There are many different versions of it, but they all follow the same general formula. First, you generate a lead. Then you qualify the prospect. Then you deliver the proposal and try to close the deal. When using a traditional funnel, it's important to know what stage a customer is at and have some plan for moving them to the next step.

That's not going to change. Instead, we're simply adding value to your message at each stage of the sales funnel you're already familiar with. We go from a broad value message then narrow that message as they move through the funnel to make it more specific to the prospect.

Now, there are three primary stages to the value message that you're going to weave into your funnel.

1. **Stage one:** showing how you deliver value (lead generation and qualifying the prospect)
2. **Stage two:** showing how other people like the prospect have achieved these benefits (aligning the proposition to them)
3. **Stage three:** showing how the prospect will achieve these benefits (proposal)

And then you close the deal.

What does it look like when you bring these three stages together? Something like this:

First, you talk about the ways that your solution delivers value to customers broadly. In other words, give them the big picture. "Our screwdrivers enable our customers to complete their construction projects faster and more efficiently."

However, since customers may derive value from your product in different ways, you then need to speak to them. If you're selling screwdrivers, you may be aware that some customers use your screwdriver as a hammer, others use it as a crowbar, and some use it to open paint cans, so you need to speak to all of the ways that customers derive value from the product.

This might require a bit of research on your existing customers. What are all of the different ways that you've seen them use your products? That's how you deliver value, not just the way you originally intended the product to be used.

With this information, you can narrow your focus to discuss how customers like the prospect achieve value. If you're talking to a carpenter, and you've seen a lot of carpenters use your screwdriver as a crowbar, then speak to that. "Many carpenters have gotten value from our product by using it as a crowbar."

Finally, align the product to the individual and share a few of the biggest ways that they will benefit from the product. "You're going to find that you complete projects between 10 to 15 percent faster, and the product will last longer than the average screwdriver, even if you use it as a crowbar, which means you'll save $100 on replacement tools over the course of a year."

So, to summarize, you're bringing a prospect into the top of your funnel and talking about all of the different ways you deliver value to customers. Then you're aligning your proposal to the prospect by sharing examples of other customers who are just like them (e.g., to a pharmaceutical company, you might say, "Here are three pharmaceutical companies who have used our supply chain solution."). Finally, you're speaking to the prospect's specific needs by sharing some of the major benefits that they will achieve as a customer.

In the end, the most important question you will answer for the prospect is "What's the ROI of investing in this product?" For example, will your product reduce their costs or increase their productivity? Calculate the actual value of those benefits and compare them with the cost to get a real number for the ROI. If that seems a bit complex, never fear. We're going to look at how you calculate ROI later in the book.

Those are the three primary stages for communicating value throughout the sales funnel, and just like the funnel itself, you start with the big picture and get narrower and more specific to the prospect along the way. These stages run alongside your regular sales funnel, weaving into your existing steps like this:

ADDING VALUE
TO THE
SALES FUNNEL

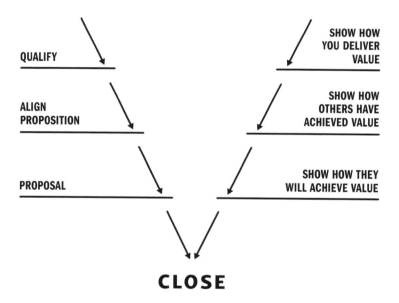

As you can see, at each stage of the sales funnel, you're going to dip into the corresponding stage in the value funnel beside it. If you do this methodically, then by the time you get to the bottom of the funnel, the customer will have a clear and compelling idea about the value that your product delivers that is specifically applicable to them. All they need now is a calculation that can provide an ROI number.

Compare that to going through the funnel in the normal way where you get to the last stage and then say, "Okay, now you need a business case so you can justify the investment, so let me bring in a value engineering team to build that case for you." And off they go into a big consulting project. With that approach, the value discussion is disconnected from the sales funnel which can actually disrupt the flow.

You may not have a value engineering team, but more and more companies use them. I've seen them disrupt as many deals as they help because they introduce new concepts and calculations apart from the sales funnel. Since you haven't introduced value into the conversation from the beginning, the business case doesn't seem believable to the prospect. You should have been giving them references and case studies all along so that value was already woven into the sales process. If you have a value team, introducing the concept of value early in the conversation will make it a lot easier for them to develop the business case since the prospect will already have an idea of the benefits they might receive.

AVOIDING YOUR NATURAL COMFORT

Why is it that salespeople tend to focus on the features of their product throughout the sales funnel and only bring in value at the very end? Why do we resist leading with value? I believe the answer is quite simple. We lead with features because that's what we know. Before you even walk into a sales meeting, you already know everything there is to know about the features of your product, so they're really easy to talk about.

You don't necessarily know what the ROI is going to be for the specific prospect you're meeting with, so it's not as easy or comfortable to talk about it. Additionally, you probably haven't been taught ROI concepts, so it's not something you can talk about confidently. It seems better to just avoid bringing it up and focus on what you know best.

And that's what the vast majority of salespeople do. They simply go through the deal and hope that the prospect doesn't ask for a business case. If they do, the sales rep will usually try to drag someone else in and hope the deal doesn't get killed in the process. This is certainly true in the world of tech sales, where I specialize, but it's a struggle common to sales in all kinds of industries. And because salespeople tend to feel more comfortable focusing on features, it also influences the marketing message. If sales is uncomfortable with value, then marketing doesn't want to promote it either, so they lead with features as well.

How do we rectify this situation? Well, if you want to communicate value, then you need to get comfortable with it. I know that seems intimidating, but it's really not that difficult. It's like flying an airplane. If you've never done it, it might seem like a complex and difficult task. But as someone who has earned his pilot's license, I can tell you from experience that flying a plane really isn't that hard once you learn the basics. You just need someone to sit down with you and show you how to do it.

That's what I'm going to do in the next few chapters. I want to take a subject that seems daunting, that can be very complex and uncomfortable, and boil it down to the basics. That way, you'll know what you need to do without having to slog through a college-level finance course. Believe it or not, building a compelling business case can be, and should be, the easiest part of the whole sales process.

There are a lot of super-intelligent, highly skilled salespeople. There's no reason why they shouldn't be able to sit down and discuss value all day long, unless they've just never been shown how to do it. No one has ever said, "Let me explain value to you so you can calculate ROI easily any time you have a sales meeting." Calculating ROI is very methodical, and I'll take you through it step by step.

I'll be bold enough to say that everything you need to know has been included in this book. First, however, you need to be able to figure out *why* a person buys. As it turns out, there are only a few basic reasons why any particular customer buys any particular product, and if you want to control the conversation and center it around value, you have to understand what that reason is.

Let's take a look at how you do that.

CHAPTER TWO

BUYING MOTIVES

Your job as a sales rep is to guide the prospect through a discussion about the benefits they're going to achieve with your product. That's it. But here's the thing: they're going to come up with the benefits themselves. You don't have to do it for them. You just have to guide them through the discussion.

As it turns out, the best way to sell something is to help the customer realize and understand the benefits they will get from your product. You are simply managing the conversation as they make these discoveries themselves.

To do this successfully, you first have to figure out "why." Why are you in front of this specific prospect? Why are they potentially buying from you? Once you can answer why, then it becomes a lot easier to guide them on their journey to understand the value they're going to achieve, the benefits they're going to get, and their ROI.

Ultimately, there are only a few buying motives that drive any sale, regardless of the prospect or the product.

Let's suppose the prospect is a company that's facing some new government regulations, and you offer a product that could potentially help them meet those regulations. In that situation, what is the real buying motive driving the company to consider your product? Well, for one thing, they're probably facing steep fines if they don't comply with the new requirements.

The CFO is going to look at the amount of the fines and weigh them against the cost of complying. In doing so, they are making a value decision. If the fines add up to about $1,000 a year but the cost of complying runs into the hundreds of thousands of dollars a year, then there's a good chance the CFO isn't going to prioritize purchasing your solution. The ROI is unclear, and there are probably a lot better ways to invest that money elsewhere.

Ultimately, if they decide to buy from you, it's going to be a sale driven by a financial motive, and if you know this going into the meeting, then you can guide them to understand the ROI through the lens of that motive. Marketing can include it in the messaging, and sales can weave it into every stage of the funnel to move the prospect across the line faster.

It's not hard to figure out *why* someone wants to buy because there are only four motives that drive people.

WHY THEY BUY

There's a lot of research on this topic, but for our purposes, any sale is ultimately driven by one of these four motives:

- Emotional
- Painful
- Obligatory
- Financial

Let's take a look at each of them.

EMOTIONAL SALE

An emotional sale is both the rarest and most difficult buying motive to deal with. An example of an emotional sale would be someone spotting a cute puppy in the window of a pet store and thinking, *Oh, my gosh, I just have to have that adorable dog!*

Puppies are cute. They're fun to play with. And when people buy a dog, they don't always sit down first and figure out what it's going to cost to take care of it for the rest of its life. My wife and I foster Huskies. They're beautiful dogs, but we had one in particular who loved to jump into the water, chew up the TV remote, and make messes everywhere he went. What's the ROI in a situation like that? Financially, it's definitely *not* a positive ROI, so why did we agree to foster him in the first place? Well, it was an emotional decision.

When you're dealing with an emotional buying motive, the sales pitch doesn't have to center around a financial ROI. Instead, it's going to be something like "Look at how awesome this sports car is. Wouldn't it be amazing to own this car and drive it around town?" In fact, there may be no possible way for that sports car to ever provide a positive ROI for the buyer, but you don't need one! In fact, it's better not to bring up the money at all. If you lead the pitch by saying, "Hey, this car is going to cost you a hell of a lot of money," then you're probably going to lose an emotional sale, no matter what ROI you try to claim.

That wild Husky was a beautiful dog, and luckily he found a permanent home, but if you looked at it from a financial perspective, then he never provided any kind of ROI. Owning him was all cost because he didn't really do anything for us. Yes, he was fun to play with, but that's hard to quantify. We loved fostering him, but it was purely emotional.

An effective sales pitch for an emotional motive is going to guide the prospect through that powerful landscape of *feelings* so they see the intangible, emotional rewards of buying. There's really no other value in the sale. In that way, an emotional buying motive is unique because there's no concrete, quantifiable value for the buyer you can use to guide the conversation.

OBLIGATORY SALE

An obligatory motive means the prospect is *required* to buy something. To use our earlier example, what if the company dealing with new regulations was facing more than just modest fines? What if they were facing fines so steep that it would put them out of business? What if they were looking at being shut down if they failed to comply within a certain time frame?

In that case, they would have no choice but to find a solution that would help them meet the demands of these new regulations.

It's an obligatory sale. They have to buy a solution, and you can use that obligation in the conversation to help them realize the ROI from your specific solution.

PAINFUL SALE

One thing we used to hear in sales all the time was "Find the customer's pain point." Many salespeople still operate this way. Let me be clear: I believe this is the single worst way to sell. Why? Because the customer may not have a pain point, and even if they do, they might not recognize that their pain point can be fixed by your product. Often, especially with technology today, *there is no pain point!* You're simply asking the customer to replace something that isn't painful for them with your product.

Let's suppose the prospect is using an old accounting system that works just fine, but you approach them to try to sell your new accounting software. Well, they don't recognize any pain point with their current software because it has met their needs thus far. Why do they need a new one? You can use value, you can use ROI, but you can't use a pain point.

When people talk about finding the customer's pain point, what they're really doing is the equivalent of setting up a table in the middle of the desert to sell water and hoping some desperate, thirsty person will walk by. This approach is as silly as trying to sell new televisions by calling every single person in your city and asking them if their current TV is broken. In my experience, that's the essence of the "finding pain points" approach to selling, and it's incredibly ineffective.

Even if a prospect is driven by some kind of pain, there's usually a value component that can guide the conversation far better. There's almost always a financial motive alongside the pain point that will make a more compelling case.

FINANCIAL SALE

Ultimately, on some level, almost every sale is a financial sale because the prospect hopes to get a return from the product you're trying to sell. So while you can appeal to other buying motives—emotional, obligatory, painful—you will never go wrong by guiding the prospect to consider their financial motive. You can even sell baby alligators wholesale as long as you make a rational business case for why raising alligators is a great financial decision.

No matter what other motives might be driving someone, the last thing they think about before deciding whether or not to buy something is some version of *Is this a good value?* Think about it. When you're considering buying a car, what's the last thing you think about before signing on the dotted line? Isn't it usually something like *Is this costing me too much? Is it worth what they're charging me? Will I get enough value out of the purchase to make it worth the investment?* In other words, in the end, you're making a financial decision, so if the salesperson can appeal to that motive, they're going to be far more likely to get you to sign.

Most of the time, you can drive a prospect to a financial motive, no matter what other buying motive may be influencing them. And once you do that, you create positive ROI, and that's always a more compelling and rational case. This is especially true if you're selling B2B and you have a two-stage process to deal with. Your point of contact needs to be able to justify the cost of your solution to a financial decision-maker, and a financial motive will do that more effectively than an emotional appeal or talking about "pain points." It also provides a more compelling case for why the company should move forward with *your* solution over *other* solutions.

Let's suppose a CEO is considering buying a brand-new corporate jet. In reality, this is almost entirely an emotional sale, and most of the time, the salesperson would try to appeal to the CEO's emotions by talking about the features: how amazing the interior is, how comfortable the seats are, and so on. But here's the thing: even if the sale is being driven mostly by the CEO's ego, the salesperson can still appeal to the financial component.

Maybe the jet will allow the CEO to travel in ways that they couldn't before, which will open up more opportunities to conduct business and grow the company in new markets. So, while it certainly has an emotional motive, there is also a financial motive. By focusing on the latter, the salesperson is going to save a lot of time and move the prospect to a sale much faster.

See how easy it is?

Let's suppose you're trying to sell someone a sports car. It's purely an emotional sale because no one actually *needs* a sports car, right? Any economy car will get you to the grocery store in the same amount of time. So what's the ROI, other than the intangible enjoyment that comes from owning a fancy car? Is there really any way you can introduce a financial component, point to an ROI number, and shorten the deal time?

Absolutely. No, you're not going to try to convince the prospect that a sports car is somehow the cheapest automobile, but you could point out that the actual "out-of-pocket" investment isn't as much as it might seem. For example, some sports cars hold their value fairly well. Often, they're reliable and, with proper maintenance, will stay in good condition for a long time. That means if your prospect decides to resell the car at some future date, they will be able recover quite a bit of the cost. You can point this out and put actual concrete numbers on this value component.

With products that hold their value well, you're not looking at the acquisition cost but the actual cost over the lifetime of the product. In the case of software, the value tends to go to zero over time, but with other products, this is not the case. For instance, if you're selling combines to farmers, then the combine has a residual value, so when the farmer decides to get rid of it, much of that value can be recovered by reselling it. Many companies buy delivery trucks with the intention of only using them for a year or two before selling them off and recovering some of the cost.

Rental car companies use a similar strategy, buying new vehicles, then selling them at a fixed mileage or point in time to reduce ongoing maintenance costs. Consequently, if you're trying to sell new vehicles to a rental company, you wouldn't look only at the acquisition cost of the vehicle to determine ROI; you would look at the total cost of the car over that fixed period, which is the acquisition cost *minus* the recovery cost.

Ultimately, you're guiding the purchase toward value components which will make it easier to get the prospect over the line. With the sports car, instead of saying, "Buy this because it's cool and it'll be fun to drive it," you're saying, "Buy this because it's actually a decent investment with good ROI because of its reliability and resale value, and yes, it's cool too." See the difference? There's still an emotional motive driving the prospect to consider buying the car, but you're introducing a financial motive alongside it as well.

Now, are there some circumstances where you *can't* or *don't* want to shift the prospect to a financial buying motive? Possibly, but in my experience, very rarely. If you're trying to get someone to buy a Husky, then it's probably going to be a purely emotional decision. What pain point could you use to get them to buy that dog? Honestly, there doesn't seem to be one. They don't feel quantifiable pain because of a lack of Huskies in their life. They're not obligated to buy the dog either.

How in the heck can you communicate ROI about the purchase of a Husky? You probably can't. You could try to make the case that the dog will save the prospect money on an alarm system by acting as a guard dog, but realistically, anyone that knows Huskies knows that the dog is more likely to be excited about playing with the intruder than trying to fend them off.

Fortunately, cases like these are the exception, not the rule. Even the most indulgent emotional purchases almost always have value components attached to them that can be highlighted in order to shorten the deal time significantly.

If you're losing deals, then you might consider if you're appealing to the right motive. Can you add a financial component to the conversation? Appeal to a financial motive (whether *instead of* or *alongside* other motives), and you will create a far stronger case for the sale every time. Whether you're selling sports cars, customer relationship management software, or high-end tractors, you can almost always find a way to appeal to a financial motive.

SHOW THEM THE MONEY

Understanding buying motives enables you to determine why someone might buy from you so you can steer the conversation around whatever value components there might be. Even if they're motivated by other things, it's always going to create a more compelling case if you appeal to a financial motive. If the customer says, "I have to solve this problem," which is an obligatory sale, it's still in your best interest to show them how your solution will reduce their risk, increase their productivity, cut costs, or whatever the financial benefits happen to be.

By showing that your solution is the most cost-effective way to solve the problem and will provide a positive ROI, you transform a painful, obligatory, or emotional decision into a financial decision. And that, in turn, shortens your time to close the deal, making it easier for the prospect to go forward.

Let's suppose a prospective company is considering building a new factory. What are the questions the CFO is going to want to answer? Probably questions like the following: How much will it cost to build this factory, and how long will it be until we recover those costs? How much potential profit can we make from the factory, and what will its useful life be? In other words, the CFO approaches it as a rational, financial decision. But we all do this far more often than we realize.

When you take some of your hard-earned money and put it into an interest-generating savings account, what do you ask yourself? Probably questions like "How much money can I afford to put in? How long will that money be tied up? What's the interest rate I'll earn on that money, and is it worth it to tie up the money in a certificate of deposit for a year at that interest rate?"

In other words, there's almost always a financial motive tied to other motives in any purchase. And by focusing on the financial component, you can turn *almost any* buying decision, no matter how emotional and irrational, into a rational decision where the customer can clearly perceive value. When you do that, the prospect will practically drive the sale themselves.

Once you've appealed to the buyer's motives and shown them the value components of the sale, you can then tie the benefits to the features of your product. By doing that, you help the customer understand how your solution is their best option for receiving those benefits.

CHAPTER THREE

FEATURES VERSUS BENEFITS

When it comes to communicating the benefits of your product, I'm going to make it very simple for you. You see, no matter what you're selling, there are only *three possible benefits*.

At this point in the sale, you should understand the prospect's motive for buying, and you should have introduced a financial component by highlighting the benefits of making the investment. Now, it's time to tie those benefits to the actual features of your product. In this chapter, we're going to look at how you do that, but first, let's go back to what I said at the beginning. Are there really only three possible benefits to any product?

That might sound like a ridiculous claim. Maybe you're thinking, *Hey, my product gives customers a lot more than three benefits!* While that may be true, ultimately, all of those benefits fall into three categories. What are they?

1. Increased productivity
2. Reduced cost
3. As a byproduct of the first two, increased profitability

That's it. Every benefit your product offers falls into one of these three categories, and if you'll think about individual benefits for a minute, you will see how. Let's suppose you're selling accounting systems. What benefits can you discuss with the prospect?

Your accounting system is going to reduce the number of accountants they need (thereby reducing cost) because the system automates a lot of tasks, and it will increase the productivity of their accountants because they will be able to generate reports far quicker. It will also increase the productivity of their managers because they will be able to see the reports from the accounting system earlier in the month and in a shorter amount of time.

Now, think about all of the benefits that you already know about your own product and see if you can't reorganize them so they fit within these three categories. In so doing, you are simplifying the sales process, giving the prospect less to consider, and making it easier to close the deal. If you're familiar with your product, then it's probably not hard to figure out how the benefits fit into these three categories.

I have an employee who takes Uber to work every day because he doesn't own a car. It costs him a lot of money, so he's been thinking about purchasing a vehicle with good gas mileage. The salesperson's natural tendency might be to use the pain strategy and point out how painful it is to take Uber every day. "Wouldn't it be easier to just take a car?" That strategy *might* help sell the call, but a far more effective strategy would look at the benefits.

Could the salesman at the car dealership appeal to these three categories of benefits? Easily! The car will both increase productivity *and* reduce costs. The cost of the car is eventually going to be cheaper than paying for Uber every single day, so it's a long-term investment that will eventually save money. Will it increase productivity? Of course. My employee will no longer have to wait for the Uber driver to show up. He can just hop in his own car and go. And together, those two benefits contribute to increased profitability, because he's going to have more money in his pocket and the ability to get to work faster and easier.

FROM BENEFITS TO FEATURES

You can do the same thing for almost any product. Take all of the benefits that your product offers customers and simplify them to these three categories. And once you've clarified the benefits, you need to connect them to the features of your product. Every feature is going to drive those benefits.

Let's use the example of the accounting software. What are the features? You could point out the user-friendly interface, the ease of integrating with your existing solutions and databases, or the different color options you have for generating reports. You can tie all of those features to either increasing the productivity of your accountants or reducing the cost for your IT department to manage the software.

You can try this same exercise with any product or service. Let's suppose you're trying to sell an inventory management system. What are the features of the product and how can you connect them to these three benefits? Well, the system tracks inventory and orders new stock at the appropriate time. That's a feature of the system, and the benefit of that feature is that the customer can reduce the amount of inventory they keep on hand, which will reduce the cost of storage and carrying costs.

Just remember, you *lead* with the benefit, then *tie it* to the feature, so you would communicate it in this way: "Our system can reduce the cost of storage by $50,000 a year (reduced cost) and reduce the amount of time your employees need to spend managing inventory reports by two to three hours per week (increased productivity) because it tracks inventory and orders new stock automatically at the appropriate time (feature)."

Whether you're selling the original product or a new version of the same product with additional features, you're ultimately doing the same thing: boiling the benefits down to these three categories and tying them to the product features.

And this isn't just an approach for sales. Marketing can do the same thing. In your marketing message, focus on how the product increases productivity, reduces cost, and increases profitability. Then show how the features of your product enable customers to achieve these benefits better than any competitor's product.

Let's suppose the company is releasing a new version of their inventory management system, and marketing wants to promote all of the improvements and additions. They might want to say something like "The new and improved version of our product will further reduce the costs for your IT department and provide productivity gains for the end user. How do we do it?" Then they can talk about some of the important new features.

Ultimately, any prospect you talk to wants an answer to the

question "What's in it for me?" They're looking for ROI on their purchase. That's why you lead with benefits. You're answering that all-important question, and then you're tying it to your product features to show *how* they're going to get those benefits.

Just remember to always *lead* with the benefits. Don't rely on the customer to figure out how your product's features are going to benefit them. Start by presenting the real value, the ROI, and then connect it to the features.

ANOTHER ROOKIE MISTAKE: REVENUE VERSUS PROFITABILITY

There's a related mistake that rookie salespeople sometimes make when presenting the benefits of their product. They talk about a change in *revenue* rather than a change in *profitability*. So let's be clear, when you lead with benefits, always look at profitability!

This is a fairly complex topic that we will cover in more depth later, but it's important to point it out now. Some salespeople lead their pitch by talking about the increase in revenue that their product can deliver, but this doesn't make a big enough impact on a prospect. Think about it. You might say you can increase their revenue by $100,000, but what if their profit margin is only 10 percent?

You think you're swinging a big sledgehammer—"Wow, we could make $100,000 in additional revenue?"—but the prospect knows that, after costs, it's only going to deliver them $10,000 in profit. Depending on the cost of your product, it may not even be enough to deliver a positive ROI. And if you're selling B2B, then it's going to be an even bigger problem when the prospect goes back to the financial decision-maker and delivers your pitch:

"So, the product can deliver us $100,000 in revenue, but that's only $10,000 in profit, and it's going to require a $70,000 investment? Doesn't sound like good ROI to me."

A change in revenue is only a benefit if you calculate the profit margin, so you might as well lead with a change in profitability to begin with. Using revenue fails to factor in the impact of the sale itself, and once the prospect or the financial decision-maker does the math, they might change their mind. In the end, a sale you thought you'd made might be derailed because you used revenue instead of profit.

I mention this now because it's such a common mistake when leading with benefits. In fact, I'll put it a bit more bluntly. Ignore revenue! Revenue is meaningless when making a sales pitch! If you use it, you're likely to hurt your business case, and you certainly won't help it. *Your business case is as weak as the weakest data point you put in*, and revenue is about the weakest data point you can use.

You want to make a strong, credible business case using impactful data points. Lead with benefits, avoid revenue, and then tie your features back to those benefits. When you do this, you make it a lot easier for the prospect to relate the benefits to the value you're going to deliver. You also make it easier to calculate the actual ROI of investing in your product, and you create a business case that is both compelling and believable to the customer.

But how can you be sure—and how can you *prove*—that your

product is likely to generate positive ROI for a customer? Well, you can actually conduct a quick assessment when you're walking into a sales meeting to determine if your product is likely to generate positive ROI for the prospect. This technique relies on two things: breadth and repeatability.

By using breadth and repeatability, you can look at any project and determine quickly if it's going to give the customer a positive or negative ROI. We'll discuss how this works next.

CHAPTER FOUR

BREADTH AND REPEATABILITY

There's a really easy way to assess if your product will deliver value even before you sit down and calculate the actual numbers. As you're walking into a potential deal, this technique can help you quickly understand exactly how to approach your value proposition and set yourself up for success. This is especially important if you know it's going to be a difficult value proposition that will require you to spend more time articulating and justifying the benefits.

The technique involves using "breadth" and "repeatability" to communicate a positive ROI. It's quite simple: the more people a product touches, and the more often it touches them, then the greater the potential ROI is going to be for the customer. That's the concept here, so let's define our terms.

When we say "breadth," we're talking about the reach of your product. How many people will be using it or affected by it?

How many users will there be within the organization that purchases it? Let's suppose a company is thinking about buying some expensive software solution. How much are they willing to invest if only a single person in the company is going to end up using that software? Probably not much. But what if every person in the company is going to use it? That's a much broader reach, and even a small benefit multiplied across a large number of employees will deliver a lot of value. In addition, it's more likely to be obvious to the buyer that the benefit exists.

If "breadth" refers to the number of people who will use or be impacted by the product, then "repeatability" refers to how often it will be used. Again, a customer is probably going to be willing to invest a lot more if they know a product will get a lot of use. To use our software example, if every salesperson in the company is going to use the software, but they're only going to use it once a year in order to collect annual sales information, then it has high breadth but low repeatability.

Or what if only a single accountant is going to use the software, but they're going to use it all day long every day? Then it has low breadth but high repeatability. In both of those examples, a positive ROI may be more difficult to achieve. But what if it's new-hire onboarding software that a single staff member will use only a few times a year? That's low breadth *and* low repeatability, and generating a positive ROI is going to be a challenge.

In all of these cases, the customer is less likely to invest a lot in the product because low breadth or low repeatability suggests low ROI. Now, if every team member is going to use the software every day to get their job done, then it has both high breadth and high repeatability—and that's your ideal. If you're walking into a sales situation where the prospect will experience both high breadth and high repeatability, then you're likely to have an easier time making a strong business case for the investment and communicating a clear ROI.

In some ways, this is unique to the customer. For example, you could sell a customer relationship management (CRM) solution to a prospective company with a hundred sales reps more easily than selling that same solution to a company with only two sales reps. So it's not your *product* that determines breadth and repeatability; it's how your prospect *intends to use* your product.

The same product can be great for one customer and terrible for another. One reason why those lists of "top products" from the big consulting firms aren't particularly helpful is because solutions deliver value uniquely for different prospects.

However, to make it as simple as possible, we can use the following equation:

Breadth × Repeatability = Value

If you can walk into a sales meeting and communicate high breadth and high repeatability, then it's going to be a whole lot easier to get the prospect to see high ROI potential. Now, here's the trick: you can adjust the way you present the product and communicate the benefits so that you *increase* the breadth and repeatability, thereby making a stronger case for ROI to the customer.

MAKING A STRONGER CASE

Let's suppose you're trying to sell onboarding automation software to a company that only has a single HR rep and only hires a few people a year. On the way into the meeting, you do a quick analysis of breadth and repeatability, and you realize they're both very low. Now, what can you do with that information? Do you give up on the sale, cancel the meeting, and go home? Absolutely not.

The purpose of the analysis is to help you adjust your presentation so you can communicate positive ROI even if breadth and repeatability are low. How do you do that? Well, you could give the prospect a huge discount and offer to sell your product for $5. That's cheap enough that positive ROI is almost guaranteed, but you'll probably go broke doing it.

There's another way. You could say something like this:

"Yes, you only hire one person a year on average, but you know how incredibly important the onboarding of that one person is. If you get it wrong, you could really hurt the company and every single team member in it. You might even get sued by the new hire. One bad hire can be catastrophic—and very expensive for everyone in the company. That's a huge amount of responsibility that hinges on your onboarding process. Doesn't it make sense to automate that process? That's what our software does—safely and securely. It's a big investment, but think about all of the money you're potentially saving by protecting yourself and the entire team from a bad hire."

An analysis of breadth and repeatability has given you a chance to adjust your message so that it still communicates positive ROI by showing how that bad hire might impact many employees. You can do this for almost any product with almost any customer in almost any situation.

COST AND CONTENT

But what do you do if you don't have any way to boost breadth and repeatability? There are two other factors you can look at: cost and content. Is there a way you can use cost to offset low breadth and repeatability? Let's suppose you're trying to sell tax filing software to a prospective client. If they don't file taxes properly, they could face some rather large fines, so there's a cost associated with *not* buying your product. You can use this to diminish the negative impact of low breadth and repeatability.

You can also use content, which is the valuable information provided by the product. Maybe you're selling a CRM system that only a single sales rep is going to use once or twice a month. Again, that's low breadth and repeatability, but you can point out the incredible value of the contact list the sales rep is building with that software. That contact list alone makes the investment worthwhile.

If you can't increase breadth or repeatability in your presentation, then look at cost and content. See how these two factors come into play, and use them to boost the perceived value of your solution.

USING THE LITMUS TEST

Breadth and repeatability (as well as cost and content) serve as a litmus test when you're about to walk into a sales meeting, so you can quickly assess how the meeting is going to go. If either breadth or repeatability are low—and especially if *both* are low—then you know it's going to be harder to communicate positive ROI to the prospect. Since you now know that, you can adjust the way you present your product's benefits so that you get the prospect to a positive ROI.

Later, we're going to look at how you calculate the actual ROI of the sale, and when we do, we'll use breadth and repeatability again to boost the numbers. However, in the meantime, it's important to have the equation in your mind: *Breadth × Repeatability = Value.* If the prospect can touch more people more often with your product, then they will perceive much greater ROI. That increases the likelihood of making the sale.

When you realize that the breadth and repeatability of your product are low, then you need *another value proposition* to justify the investment. If possible, try to find ways to increase breadth and repeatability, and if you can't do that, use cost and content. In our earlier example, only one HR staff member was going to use the software a few times a year, so we boosted breadth and repeatability by tying that infrequent one-person use of the onboarding software to the overall performance of the company so that it touched every team member all the time. We communicated the financial danger of making a bad hire and presented our software as a solution that would safely and securely automate the hiring process.

Suddenly, a product that one person will use infrequently becomes a product that everyone will be impacted by all the time, which makes it an important investment all year long. This isn't some kind of trick, and we're not lying to the prospect. There really is a direct connection between the hiring of new staff and the overall financial performance of the company. We're simply adjusting the presentation to point this out so we can get the prospect to recognize the positive ROI from your solution.

Let's look outside of the world of business software. What if you're trying to sell a new harvesting combine to a farmer. A quick breadth and repeatability analysis tells you that only one person is going to use it, and that farmer is only going to use it a couple of times each season. Since breadth and repeatability are both low, it might be hard for the prospect to see a positive ROI. Even if the farmer is still willing to buy the combine, they might ask for a steep discount before they're willing to sign on the dotted line.

To overcome that, you can point out that the farmer will have greater efficiency, thanks to the various features of the combine, which will enable them to harvest many more acres each season. While they're still only using it at harvest time, they will touch more acres, which will enable them to provide more of their produce to more people. In this case, you've pointed out that the greater productivity, even for just one person, generates significand benefit. You've increased the repeatability not in the number of times used but in the number of acres that can be harvested in the same time frame. That makes it easier for the farmer to see positive ROI, and that, in turn, allows you to sell the combine for more money.

If you're selling a super-expensive corporate jet to a CEO, you have low breadth because there are only a few seats on the plane. The CEO just can't fit that many people on the plane, *but* maybe the company can fly *more often* to *more places* by owning their own jet. Suddenly, the repeatability is a whole lot bigger, and the value seems a whole lot greater to the prospect.

You can do this same exercise with practically any product or service. Before you walk into a sales meeting, conduct a quick mental analysis of the breadth and repeatability of the product to determine how difficult it's going to be to communicate a positive ROI to the prospect. If breadth or repeatability are low, then you know in advance that you're going to adjust the value proposition to get the prospect to positive ROI somehow.

There are some other mental techniques you can use to organize your thoughts and strengthen your message before you talk to the prospect. Let's look at a few of those in the next chapter. After all, you largely win or lose the sale before you ever make your final presentation.

CHAPTER FIVE

PREPPING FOR THE FIRST MEETING

Every company that sells a product believes their product delivers value. If they didn't, they wouldn't be in business.

I have a friend who runs a company that makes and sells, among other things, frozen meatballs. At first glance, the value component of his product might not be clear, but his company delivers a high-quality product at a reasonable price. For many customers, buying the ingredients to make their own meatballs and then spending time making them at home is actually more expensive than buying my friend's prepackaged product. That makes it a value sale with clear benefits: reducing cost and increasing productivity.

You don't have to be cheaper to deliver more value. You only have to deliver a *greater ratio of value to cost* to be competitive in the market. Whether you're in sales or marketing, understanding the value your solution delivers is the first step toward presenting the benefits and ROI effectively to the customer.

Consider this. Everyone talks about building a better mousetrap, but when you create a better mousetrap, it's really hard to communicate a better value-to-cost ratio. Why? Because the appeal of a traditional mousetrap is that it's incredibly cheap and your better design can't possibly be any cheaper. That's why most "new and improved" mousetraps try to make an emotional appeal by saying things like "touch-free disposal," or "more humane."

In other words, instead of trying to claim that the product has greater value, they turn it into an emotional sale that appeals to the "yuckiness" of dealing with traditional mousetraps. But no prospect has an emotional attachment to a better mousetrap, so it's always going to be harder to sell. It's not that you can't improve on the mousetrap's traditional design, but it's hard to change the value ratio of your new-and-improved product when compared to the value ratio (namely, the very low cost) of a traditional mousetrap.

It's important to keep all of this in mind when you're headed into your first sales meeting with a prospect because a little preparation will go a long way toward closing the deal. Remember one thing above all else: walk into *every* deal with a value message *first*!

Let's suppose you're taking an elevator up to an office suite where you're meeting a prospect to pitch them on your product. That short elevator ride is all the time you need to prepare yourself for the meeting. There are a few techniques you can use to make the most of that time, and once you understand these techniques and get good at them, it's going to be very easy for you to figure out the value message you need to lead with.

TECHNIQUE #1: WHAT THE CUSTOMER WANTS

In over a thousand case studies that I've conducted, one thing has always been absolutely true: there are only one or two benefits that drive any deal, and two or three benefits that support it. And that's it.

While there may be more than five benefits, there are never *more* than five that influence the decision, and usually one or two that *make* the decision. What does this mean for you as a sales rep? It means you can focus on those two main benefits. Remember the guy who was taking Uber to work every day? What benefits drove his decision to finally buy his own vehicle? First, and most importantly, that it would save him money over the long term. Second, that it would save him time getting to and from work.

There are probably dozens of other benefits to owning his own vehicle. He can set the temperature to something he prefers so he's more comfortable. He can probably get a date easier now. He has more flexibility in making plans. And so on. You could create a huge list of benefits, but ultimately, his decision to buy a car was driven by just two things. If you focus on those two things, you will close the deal.

Adding all of those other benefits into the conversation won't make the sales pitch stronger. Actually, you'll probably weaken the deal psychologically by giving the prospect more to think about and giving yourself more to prove. Focus on the benefits that are big enough to sway the deal, and don't worry about the rest.

You already know all of the different value points of your product, so the first thing you need to do is narrow that list down to two or three benefits that are likely to make an impact on the customer. You should have some idea of why this particular prospect is meeting with you. What are they looking for? Do they want to increase the productivity of their sales reps? Do they want to increase the yield on their acres, or expand the number of acres they're covering?

Identify the two or three benefits they are likely looking for, and from that list, select the benefits you're going to emphasize to match their goals. Remember, each of these benefits will fall under one of three categories (reducing cost, increasing productivity, increasing profitability). Use breadth and repeatability to get an idea of the best way to communicate a greater potential ROI. You should be able to do all of this in just a few minutes before meeting with a prospect and making your pitch.

If you're in marketing instead of sales, you can use the same technique to focus your messaging on a target audience. What is the audience looking for, which of the benefits of your product will most significantly help them achieve those goals, and how can you use breadth and repeatability to communicate a greater positive ROI through your messaging?

You should already have some sense of how the customer is likely to achieve value through your solution, so instead of trying to use everything, focus on a few things that really matter to them. Don't make the mistake that many sales reps make of trying to throw absolutely everything at the wall and hoping that something will stick.

Focus on the few things that matter most to the customer, specifically the two or three benefits that will best help them achieve their goals, and create a value proposition that speaks to these things directly. This is the first and most important technique.

TECHNIQUE #2: DRIVE IT TO A FINANCIAL MOTIVE

The second technique is to figure out how you can drive the sale to a financial buying motive, even if there are other motives influencing the customer. In Chapter Two, we identified four possible motives for why a prospect might decide to buy: emotional, painful, obligatory, and financial. As I said then, it is almost always easier to make a financially motivated sale because it creates a rational, numbers-based sale, and in my experience, you will always win a numbers-based sale.

You can show value and still not win an emotional sale because emotions can be irrational. However, you can often take an emotional sale and make it a financial sale. Make it about the numbers, not the feelings!

How do you do this? Well, it's not difficult, no matter what the prospect is buying or why. Ultimately, the customer is considering this product because they're trying to achieve *something*. How does that goal translate into a numbers-based goal? Are they trying to increase productivity, reduce cost, or increase profit?

If you can connect the customer's goal to a few benefits that provide real numbers, then you can guide them to a financial motive for buying the product. Again, use breadth and repeatability so you can increase those numbers to something that communicates a clear ROI. There are always at least a few ways you can explain the benefits of a product that highlight either breadth or repeatability.

To use an earlier example, let's suppose you're trying to sell a new, expensive combine to a farmer, and you run the numbers and discover that a positive ROI is going to be difficult to achieve if they only use the combine on a single field. Expand the presentation to three or four fields and see if that doesn't get you to a positive ROI.

Once you're in the meeting, don't just listen to the customer's words. Try to perceive their real motivation. What are they trying to accomplish? What are concrete numbers-based goals that they hope to achieve to make the investment worthwhile? Adjust your value message accordingly.

Let's suppose you're selling a software solution, and the customer has told you, "We need to deploy *some* solution because employee satisfaction is way down." After a bit of discussion, it becomes clear that this is largely a consequence of their current software solution being clunky and inefficient. While this can be viewed as an obligatory (or possibly emotional) sales motive, in your pitch you can talk about the financial impact of reducing the burden on employees. Point out how much easier your solution will be for them and how it's going to drive greater productivity through increased efficiency.

With a bit of calculation, you can come up with a few concrete numbers attached to these benefits. This takes what might otherwise be an obligatory or emotionally driven sale and turns it into a numbers-driven financial sale.

TECHNIQUE #3: CHALLENGE YOUR PRECONCEIVED NOTIONS

Remember, the key is to speak to how *this specific prospect* is going to achieve value, not how you *intend* your product to deliver value. Two different customers might derive value from the same product in very different ways. Maybe your product wasn't specifically designed to boost employee satisfaction. It doesn't matter. If that's what this prospect hopes to achieve, and you can get them there with your solution, then speak to that.

A prospect wants to know how your product delivers value, but when you communicate it, you need to match the value you deliver to what they're hoping to achieve. Of course, you're not limited to that. You can also share other ways that your product delivers value, but stay focused. Never use a shotgun approach. If you dump every single possible way your product can deliver value to a prospect, you diminish the value of all of it.

Ideally, you should create a value proposition around *two or three things* that matter to the prospect and give them a very clear idea of why it's a good idea to move forward with your solution. Don't add more than three, because you have to justify every reason you give the prospect. If you give them ten reasons why they should buy your product, then you have to find a numbers-driven way to justify all ten. That's not going to be easy. If you limit it to just three, then you can still make a big impact, and it's going to be a lot easier to justify the actual value of those three things.

Ultimately, you have to challenge your own preconceived notions about your product. Walk into the sales meeting with an open mind about how your product delivers value. Yes, you already know *what* your product does, but you may not yet have a clear sense of how specific customers derive value from it.

So ask them. Ask the prospect what they're trying to achieve and how they think your product can help them achieve it. *This is how you guide them to discover the value for themselves.* Then talk about the value your product delivers from that perspective. You should already have some sense of this before you walk into the meeting, so try to prepare your value message in advance, tailoring it to this specific prospect's goals.

QUESTIONS FOR THE ELEVATOR RIDE

- Which two or three benefits are likely to make the biggest impact on the prospect?

- How does the prospect want to derive value from the product?

- Does this project have the potential for a high return on investment?

- If the ROI potential seems low, how can you boost breadth or repeatability to get a higher ROI?

- How can you drive the prospect to a financial buying motive and present concrete numbers to justify the sale?

A LITTLE PREPARATION GOES A LONG WAY

No matter what you're selling, or who you're selling to, the most important thing you can do is to prepare a little bit before meeting with a prospect. There are so many things that can derail a sales opportunity, but the biggest one is failing to talk about how you're going to deliver value up front.

Your value proposition starts with the very first sentence you say to the prospect, so make value a theme from the very beginning, not just one point at the end of the funnel. If you haven't listened to what the customer is saying, if you don't have a sense of how they want to achieve value, then you can't speak to the benefits that will make the biggest impact.

Remember, if you're selling B2B, then you often have to sell your product twice. First, you're selling it to your point of contact, and then that person has to sell it to someone else in senior management who holds both the budget and signing authority. That makes it even more important to give them a business case that resonates powerfully with how they want your product to deliver value.

Focus on two or three big benefits that the customer can really wrap their heads around. This is going to make it easier for that prospect to become an internal champion for your project. You have to win against other projects that are competing for the same money, so the tighter and cleaner you make the message, the better your chances are going to be. Concrete numbers always win the day!

Listen, it's not that hard. You're probably already very well acquainted with your product, and you probably already listen carefully to your prospects and customers. So you should be able to assess what the most impactful benefits are and adjust your value message in just a few short minutes before you meet with someone.

One effective way of starting with value is to open your meeting by sharing some examples of existing customers in the same industry who have similar goals to the prospect: "We have another customer in your industry who was looking to expand the acreage that they were currently using on their farm, and this is how they did it."

By starting with tangible examples, you underscore the benefits right away and put yourself in a winning posture from the very beginning of the meeting. Eventually, however, you do have to get to those concrete numbers. You can't just tell a prospect, "Your team members are going to be a lot more productive." You need to do actual calculations that get the prospect to some concrete ROI number. I know a lot of sales reps find this daunting.

Well, here's the good news: it's a lot easier than it seems. In the next chapter, we're going to take a look at the financial metrics and learn some easy calculations you can make to get those numbers. So don't be scared of the financial metrics. You can calculate the numbers a lot quicker and more easily than you realize. Let's find out how.

CHAPTER SIX

FINANCIAL METRICS

A lot of people are scared of financial metrics, and I don't blame them. Calculating the actual ROI of your product and coming up with concrete numbers that you can share with a prospect is a daunting undertaking, but I'm telling you from experience— my own experience and the experiences of the thousands of salespeople I've trained and worked with—*financial metrics aren't difficult.*

They are, however, precise. What makes them *seem* complicated is that they're often taught like an academic course rather than a practical course. Well, we're going to take a practical approach, and the good news is, you probably use ROI metrics every day and just don't realize you're doing it. Why should you be afraid of something you're already doing every day?

To use an earlier example, flying an airplane probably seems incredibly complicated if you've never been taught how to do it, but if I showed you how the controls work, you'd realize it's actually not that hard. In fact, I bet almost anyone could fly a plane after just a single lesson. The landing might take a bit of practice, but while you're up in the air, it's pretty simple.

Dare I say, flying an airplane isn't rocket science, and neither is understanding financial metrics. And once you understand the metrics, you can build and deliver a compelling business case that is both rational and logical, with *real* ROI.

So let's take a look at the most important financial metrics.

RETURN ON INVESTMENT (ROI)

Return on investment (ROI) is a very straightforward metric, and it's one you've almost certainly already used today. If you put money in a bank account that accrues interest, then you made a decision based on ROI. Let's suppose it's a savings account with a 10 percent interest rate, and you invested $100. You know you're getting $10 on that money at the end of the year, so investing in the account has a $10 return on investment. You already know this, which is why you feel safe and confident handing your $100 over to the bank.

Your job as a sales rep (or marketer) is to get the prospect to see the positive ROI they can achieve from investing in your product. Now, in my industry, which is mostly software solutions, it's best to communicate long-term value by using a *three-year horizon for achieving ROI*. A software solution is a big investment up front, so the prospect might not get to a positive ROI after one year, or even two. By using a three-year horizon, you smooth out any irregularities during that first year and shift the prospect's focus to the long-term investment.

Three years works best because it's usually the shortest horizon for realizing long-term ROI. Going further, to four or five years, doesn't generally make the ROI better, and a customer is going to get frustrated if they haven't achieved an average ROI by the third year. In fact, most of the time, if they haven't gotten a positive ROI by year three, they're never going to get it.

So, making an ROI estimate beyond year three is not helpful, but going shorter than that will usually decrease the ROI due to up-front costs. That makes three years the best horizon for calculating the return on investment for the customer. We're still looking at an annual ROI, but we're taking into account early costs that may impact value.

That $100 you put in the bank, what if you didn't look at it until the end of year three, and when you did, you found that you'd gained $30? You might not have noticed that you only received $4 in year one followed by $13 in the second and third years. The total is still $30, and the average return you received during that period was 10 percent per year. Similarly, if you've ever invested in the stock market or in a mutual fund, you know the daily ups and downs level out when you look at the return over the long term.

To determine the average ROI over a three-year period, you calculate the net benefit (the total benefit minus the cost) for year one, year two, and year three, add them together, and divide by three to get an average net benefit. Then divide that average by the initial cost to calculate ROI.

This is what it looks like as an equation:

$$\text{ROI} = \left\{ \frac{\text{YEAR } 1 + \text{YEAR } 2 + \text{YEAR } 3}{} \right\} \div 3$$

$$\overline{\text{INITIAL COST}}$$

That's it. That's the ROI you're going to communicate to the prospect.

Let's use our previous example. You put $100 in an interest-generating account; that's your initial investment. You estimate that you have an additional $4 in the account by the end of the first year. Since there was no need to put additional money into the account in the first year, you get a benefit of $4, less $0 additional cost, giving you a net benefit of $4 for the first year. You do that same for the second year and get a net benefit of $13. Finally, you get a net benefit of $13 for the third year. That gives you a total net benefit of $30 over three years. Now, divide that by three, and you get an average benefit of $10 per year. Finally, divide that total by the initial cost ($10 ÷ $100) to get an ROI of 0.1 (or 10 percent).

It's no more complicated than that. I've seen a lot of ways that people calculate ROI poorly, but this is *the only right way to do it.* Forget "risk-weighted ROI," "risk-adjusted ROI," or any other form of ROI that includes additional complications. There is no special methodology for ROI!

When a caveman ten thousand years ago looked out of his cave entrance at the deep snow that had accumulated, he did a quick

ROI calculation to determine if it was worth going out there to hunt.

"How hungry am I, and how likely am I to die in the snow?"

That's a simple ROI calculation. Maybe he even painted the ROI calculation on the cave wall, depicting the mammoth he wanted to eat, the spears, and the hunting party. If a caveman can do ROI calculations, so can you.

PAYBACK PERIOD

Payback period, otherwise called "time to value," simply refers to the length of time until the customer covers their costs. It's one of the best metrics, and in my experience, it's actually more impactful than ROI because it's even easier to wrap your head around. For example, you could tell the prospect that the ROI is 300 percent, or you could tell them that the payback period is four months. The latter is a lot easier for them to grasp than the former.

Any decision-maker can understand four months. They might feel good about 300 percent ROI, but four months to payback is a lot clearer:

"Okay, I will cover my initial costs in four months. That's not too bad."

Most financial decision-makers are risk averse, so they're usually looking at the payback period anyway. They want to know how long it's going to take for their investment in a product to pay them back. For example, let's suppose I'm a small plumbing contractor, and I purchase a new truck for a new employee I'm hiring. How much work will that new employee need to do before they've not only covered their own salary expense but also the cost of purchasing that truck? That's the payback period, and once I get to that point, everything moving forward becomes positive.

Since a prospect is probably thinking about the payback period anyway, it's a very strong metric. If you're trying to sell your product to a company, and the payback period is three months, then it makes little sense for them to debate the purchase for six months because they would already have covered their costs by then. Therefore, if a prospect delays making a purchase, you can point them back to the payback period and say, "You know, you would already be enjoying a $10,000-a-month benefit if you'd decided to buy when we first met because you would be past the payback period by now."

A WORD OF CAUTION

Don't add up all of the benefits during the first three years, divide the total by all of the costs during the three years, and call it ROI. If you do that, you're actually calculating the cost-to-benefit ratio, not the return on investment. This is a common mistake in a lot of marketing material and a fair number of business cases. You might get past your champion, but no financial professional will treat that type of calculation seriously if you submit it. If you've ever wondered why a deal stalled, this might have been the problem.

That lets the prospect know that every additional month they delay making the purchase is essentially costing them $10,000 in lost benefits. And that can be a powerful motivator for getting a prospect to take that final step over the line.

Payback period also gives you an easy way to unseat an existing product. To use our software example, a prospect might tell you, "We already have an application that we've been using for ten years, and it works just fine."

Here's how you can respond to this:

"Yes, absolutely, your existing product has served you well and covered its cost a long time ago, but I'm offering you something that will give you a greater ROI than what you're currently getting. The payback period is just four months, so within four months, you will have covered the initial cost, and you'll be enjoying that greater ROI."

You're not trying to convince them that their current solution is bad. It was a great purchase when they made it back in the day, but it has long since covered its cost, and it's time for the customer to move on to something that's even better. This tactic works very well. In fact, you've probably been swayed by it yourself many times. It's the reason why we all buy new smartphones every year or two.

Think about the last time you bought a new phone. Your old phone was probably still working just fine, and in your mind, you had already received enough value to cover its initial cost. So why did you buy a new one? Because you perceived greater value in the newer model, and you believed the benefits you'd received from the old phone had already outweighed its cost. Additionally, you believed that the payback period for the new phone was short enough to justify the purchase. Unless of course you lost your phone, then this was a painful sale and there was no need to look at ROI.

So if you need to unseat an existing product in order to convince a prospect to replace it with your solution, and if you want to speed up the decision-making time, show them how long it will be until they feel comfortable with their investment. You can even adopt a negative approach and say something like "Even if you deploy our solution and throw it away after the payback period, you will still get a positive ROI."

Either way, payback period is a metric that will almost always reduce the perceived risk of investing in your product. It's perfect for a prospect who is thinking about delaying their buying decision, because it shows them that a delay doesn't make financial sense, and even if there's a chance that something better will come along in two years, it's still a good idea to go forward with your product because they're still going to realize ROI soon enough to make it a good investment.

PAYBACK
PERIOD

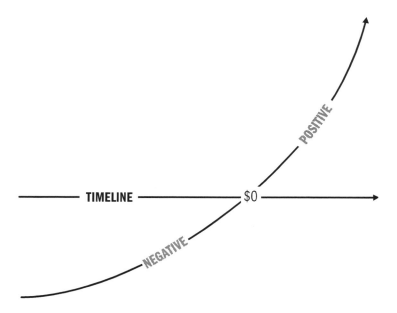

Remember the farmer who was thinking about buying that nice, expensive combine from you? The farmer knows there's a good chance that they will replace it in five years with a newer model, but if the payback period is one year, then they also know they'll get enough ROI from the combine to make it worthwhile during those five years. In five years, they could park your combine and let it rust, and they would still be okay. The increased efficiency of the combine will have made them a lot of extra money after the payback period, so it was a smart investment.

In sales, everyone is going to talk about ROI, but I encourage you to *start with payback period*, then follow it up with ROI. For example, you might say something like "This project will cover its cost in four months and deliver a 300 percent ROI."

Payback period and ROI (in that order) are the best financial metrics. They're effective, build a compelling business case, and shorten the decision-making time. In fact, they're the only real financial metrics you need.

THE UGLY ONES

Besides ROI and payback period, there are some other financial metrics that are sometimes used, but I call them "the ugly ones." You might need to understand them, but you don't need to use them. What are they? Let's take a look at a few.

NET PRESENT VALUE (NPV)

Net present value is a way to move money around in time. More specifically, it shows how much money a project or investment will gain (or lose) over time in terms of today's money. For example, $100 subjected to an annual 15 percent interest rate will be worth about $152 in three years, so $100 today is just as good as $152 three years from now.

Net present value allows you to take the money from that future date and understand what the value is at the present time. So, if you're talking about the benefits of a product on a three-year horizon, you would calculate the benefits for each year, then determine the NPV of those future benefits in today's money using some expected interest rate. Add those three numbers together, and you get the current NPV of the project for the first three years.

Frankly, this may be financially correct, but it's not a good metric for influencing decision-making. I recommend avoiding it altogether because it's not going to help you move a prospect forward.

Let's suppose you give me $100, and I give you back $30 a year for three years. Now if you just look at that, you can see the $30 return on that $100 investment delivers a 30 percent annual ROI. We know the project has a positive ROI, but let's suppose you use NPV to calculate the value of that money in terms of today's money. If you follow the NPV calculation and add up today's value of $30 for each of the three years at the 15 percent interest rate, you'll have $30 from the first year, plus $26 from the second year, and $23 from the third year. That means the net present value of that future $90 in payments will be $79 today.

So you invested $100 now, but you'll only get $79 in value back in today's money. That makes it seem like the project is negative.

The problem is, sometimes a project that is *obviously* good will give you a negative NPV. Why? Because you missed one important factor: the calculation failed to take into account the residual value of that initial $100. In most cases there's really no way to accurately calculate residual value, which means net present value will always show a project as being worse than it actually is. Indeed, NPV is not meant to calculate the value of a project; it's simply meant to move money from one point in time to another.

NPV

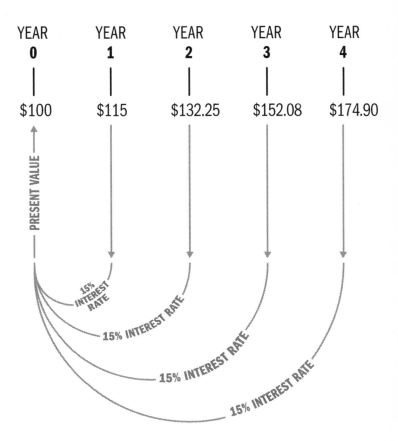

YEAR 0	YEAR 1	YEAR 2	YEAR 3	YEAR 4
$100	$115	$132.25	$152.08	$174.90

PRESENT VALUE

15% INTEREST RATE

15% INTEREST RATE

15% INTEREST RATE

15% INTEREST RATE

Remember our caveman staring out at the snowy landscape and trying to decide if he should go out in the hostile weather and hunt? He's going to use ROI to determine if the potential meat he could get is worth the risk, and he's going to use payback period to predict how long he might have to hunt out in that winter wasteland before he gets enough meat to make it worthwhile. You know what he's *not* going to use? Net present value. If he does, he'll starve.

Don't waste your time with NPV. Payback period and ROI are all you need to make your product seem worth the investment to a prospect.

INTERNAL RATE OF RETURN (IRR)

Internal rate of return is probably the most flawed financial metric, but I see a lot of people using it. They see the word "return" and think it's the same as ROI. Well, it's not. In fact, IRR has nothing to do with the return on investment of a product.

Put simply, IRR is the interest rate that sets the net-present-value calculation to zero. That's all it is. It doesn't help a prospect understand the value of investing in your product, and in fact, it's a dangerous metric that can be misused by people to justify projects that really shouldn't go forward. The truth is, you can make tiny adjustments to the time horizon or the timing of payments that seem insignificant in order to dramatically swing the internal rate of return and make a bad project seem amazing.

Many years ago, I encountered a situation in which a prominent consulting company had built an IRR model for a project that made it look like it would work. However, when we examined the calculation, we discovered that they'd generated an IRR value that was just good enough to get the project approved, but it used an odd nine-year time horizon. In fact, as we discovered, they had front-loaded the project and extended the time horizon to a ludicrous degree to make the IRR artificially higher. This magnified the value of the project, but in reality, the project was terrible and the government agency that bought the application would never experience a positive ROI.

Here's a good rule of thumb: if you're thinking about buying something and the sales rep presents an IRR calculation, stop talking to them immediately and walk away. That's how bad of a metric it is.

Is IRR good for anything? Well, IRR is the interest rate that sets the NPV to zero, so it could be useful if a project has a defined beginning and end. For instance, if you're a contractor working on a building, then you're probably getting progress payments from the owner. You have money going out and money coming in. There are going to be times during the course of the project when more money will go out than come in, so you need a certain amount of money from the bank to ensure you never go to zero.

Let's say you run a calculation and find out that you need $3 million from the bank to get to the end of this project. You can't negotiate on the loan amount; you need the $3 million to pay your employees, so less won't work. That means the interest rate on that loan is critical to you making or losing money on this project. An IRR calculation tells you that at 7 percent, for example, the NPV is zero. In other words, if the bank charges you 7 percent, you'll reach the end of this project at zero, losing nothing but walking away with nothing. If the interest rate is higher than that, then you'll lose money on the project. If it's lower, then you'll make money.

In that case, the IRR calculation plays a useful role in helping you negotiate on the rate for the loan the bank offers you.

However, when it comes to assessing the value of investing in a product, it is entirely useless and should be avoided at all costs.

TOTAL COST OF OWNERSHIP (TCO)

Total cost of ownership is a popular metric when people are assessing a technology solution. A prospect might have a clear sense of what their up-front cost is going to be, but TCO provides them with an analysis of what the up-front costs *and* the total ongoing costs are going to be.

I've seen a number of projects where TCO wasn't taken into consideration, and it caused problems. For example, maybe there were three phases to the project, but only the cost of phase one was taken into consideration when making the buying decision. And maybe there were increasing costs in phases two and three.

For sales, TCO might be important, especially if your product offers a lower cost than other products, but it will always turn the discussion toward cost. And the less your prospect pays for your product, the better the TCO is going to be. So when you bring up TCO, you also bring up the prospect of discounting. People are going to ask questions like "How much are you willing to discount the cost of the product in order to reduce my TCO and increase my benefits?" That makes it a dangerous metric for you.

It's not a good metric for helping a prospect choose between your product and an existing product. If two products have a similar TCO, which one is the prospect going to choose? The easiest option is to choose neither of them, but what if one product is a tiny bit cheaper? Will the prospect choose that one over the other? Not necessarily.

If you're getting gas for your car, and you can choose between the gas station you're used to visiting or a generic-branded gas station across the street that is selling gas for two cents per gallon less, which one are you going to choose? Probably the one you're already familiar with. While prospects can be sensitive to price, they also tend to stick with a certain caliber of recognizable brands or brands that they trust rather than going for the absolute cheapest.

For some products, this may not be the case. With a rental car, all bets are off. The customer will usually go for the cheapest. But what about food, clothing, pet supplies, bottled water? There are plenty of things where "cheapest" is not a driving factor. It may be *one* factor, but it's usually weighted against the benefits of the product. Almost every buyer is looking for the greatest *value* given the budget that they have.

Therefore, TCO is something you need to be aware of but not necessarily something that's going to drive the deal forward. You might help the prospect understand the TCO and that it is within a reasonable range, but don't lead with it unless you're absolutely the cheapest solution out there. If you *do* lead with it, just remember, it puts you up against the "buy nothing" option.

OTHER METRICS

There are numerous other financial metrics besides the ones mentioned here, but most of them are made up by consultants and usually presented in deep voices around conference tables to people who pretend to understand them. Ultimately, ROI and payback period are the only two financial metrics that you need to know. They've been around since the beginning of time, and they haven't changed.

Everything else on the face of the earth has evolved, but ROI and payback period have remained the same. They are the same calculations people have been making since we lived in caves, so don't reinvent them!

Some companies use something called "risk-weighted ROI," where they take the estimated benefits and discount them back by an estimated risk weighting. For example, let's suppose you invest $100 up front with an expected return of $30 a year. Risk weighting would take each year of a three-year horizon and weight the expected ROI based on the risk of the project during that year.

It's unnecessary to stack metrics like this. It doesn't make the product more appealing to the buyer, and it doesn't help get them over the line. ROI by itself is *already* a measure of risk. Don't bother trying to calculate future risk and then modify the ROI accordingly. That's silly.

Never combine metrics! Let metrics stand by themselves. Let's suppose someone is trying to sell you bonds, and you've assessed your risk tolerance at 10 percent. When you mention this, they tell you, "Well, we've risk weighted it to 10 percent, so you're good." Well, that doesn't tell you anything except that they have adjusted the risk based on *their* assessment, not yours. Any smart investor would want more information on the organization issuing the bonds to make their own assessment of risk before they invest.

As a salesperson, just don't do it. Don't combine metrics. I'll say it again: stick to ROI and payback period. They are all you need! That said, you're not there to teach the prospect finance. If the prospect insists on using IRR and it works out, just hand them the contract, smile, and move on. But your job as a sales rep is to sell the product, and you don't need complicated metrics to do that.

If you don't believe me, just look at banks. Banks don't use NPV or IRR or any other strange metrics. What do they use? ROI and payback period. And that's it. You'll never see the "risk weighting" on the deposit rate they have on the poster in the bank lobby.

Do exactly what the caveman did. Lead with payback period and follow up with ROI. That's how you keep a sale moving toward the finish line.

CHAPTER SEVEN

ASSESSING COSTS

Costs are usually easy to understand, easy to calculate, and less subject to debate. Most of the time, everyone will readily agree on the cost side of the calculation because it's clearer and simpler. Let's take a look at how you can assess the costs of your product or service so you can then communicate the value.

When counting the cost, there are a few things to keep in mind.

First, count every cost that is directly associated with the product. When in doubt about whether or not something is a cost, here's a simple mental test: if it takes money out of the customer's pocket, it's a cost.

Second, costs are either *one-time* or *recurring*. A one-time cost happens once, and recurring costs are ongoing. One-time costs would include things like set-up fees, acquisition fees, and even the cost of personnel to set up the product, get it running, and conduct training. Ongoing costs might include licensing fees and subscription fees. That's pretty straightforward. Just make sure you keep these two things separate.

Third, when you lay out the costs for your product, you're going to use a three-year horizon and present them as (1) initial cost, (2) year one costs, (3) year two costs, and (4) year three costs. Then break them down into one-time costs and recurring costs. If you're selling a subscription product, assume they'll pay in full on the day just before the next year starts. That may not be how they're actually paying, but it will give you an accurate ROI calculation.

Remember, you're only looking at ROI over three years. If the customer is getting financing, lay the financing out over three years. If they're paying for everything up front, you should *still* lay it out over three years. Any kind of prepayment or postpayment is essentially just another form of financing, so for the purposes of the ROI calculation, spread it out across the initial payment, year one, year two, and year three.

LAYING OUT THE COST

In general, when you're trying to determine the full cost of a product or service for a prospect, there are five categories of cost to consider:

- Software
- Hardware
- Personnel
- Consulting
- Training

While these broad-based categories may seem unique to software products, they really aren't. Many items that you purchase these days have both a software component and a hardware component. For example, many new cars come with an annual subscription for software that allows you to do things like remotely starting the vehicle. When a company buys a new truck, it may come with a software tracker.

Using these categories, you should be able to cover almost every situation. Remember, there are both one-time and recurring costs, and they need to be listed and communicated to the prospect separately. Spread them out across that three-year time horizon in order to communicate ROI more effectively. Let's look at each category of cost.

SOFTWARE

This includes all software purchased for a project, as well as any associated licensing fees and maintenance costs. To calculate the costs, you need to decide what date the sale or project begins. With some products, this is fairly straightforward. The starting date is the day the customer starts using the product. With others, especially complex products like SaaS software systems, selecting a specific starting date is a bit more open-ended. However, you need to choose a starting date so you can then look forward to that three-year horizon for costs and ROI.

Your starting date is where you put all of the initial costs, including every cost that came before that date. Everything afterward is considered year one. Now, to be clear, if all of the costs of your product are at the back end, that doesn't mean you should put them all in the "year three" category, because back-end costs are actually just another form of financing. It's a way of saying, "You owe this now, but you can pay it later."

When calculating the total cost of your product for the customer, include those back-end fees as initial costs for calculating the business case. With SaaS products in particular, anything that is a license fee goes in the initial year, year one, and year two categories. The same goes for maintenance fees. Don't put them in year three, because that's actually a payment for the fourth year of service, and you're only going to be looking at a three-year horizon.

Anything that involves financing up front should be spread out over the three years because the customer is paying all of that money up front in order to use the product over the years. Be sure to allocate the costs to the proper years, keeping in mind that the goal is to build an accurate and compelling business case for the sale.

HARDWARE

The other categories of cost follow the same basic pattern as software with a few exceptions. With hardware, the main cost issues are (1) what hardware are they buying up front, (2) will they have to buy additional hardware to support it in the future, and (3) will there be any maintenance costs on the hardware?

Selling a new combine? Here's where you put the initial cost of acquisition and any recurring maintenance and support fees in each of the future years.

CALCULATING SOFTWARE COSTS

- Select a starting date and put all initial costs on that starting date, including every cost that came before that date.

- Include back-end fees as initial costs.

- Licensing fees and maintenance fees go in the initial, year one, and year two categories. Don't put them in year three.

- Up-front financing should be spread out over the three years.

PERSONNEL

Personnel costs refer to the total number of hours of internal personnel time that will be needed to support the initial deployment, ongoing support, and management of the product. In other words, how many people will need to be on the project initially to get everything up and running? Will there be integration costs or any additional expenses using internal personnel? How many people will the customer need on an ongoing basis to manage this project? For example, if the prospective company is an airline, how many employees will they need to add to the maintenance staff to maintain that new airliner they plan to add to their fleet?

To determine the personnel costs, multiply the "fully loaded" cost by the number of hours they plan to work on the project.*

---

* The fully loaded cost includes all of the costs that make up a staff cost, including property, HR, and legal costs.

If you're not sure what the fully loaded cost is, a good rule of thumb is to set it as 35 percent over the average salary.

CONSULTANTS

If the prospect will be using consultants or outside help (for training, integration, etc.), then you need to determine the up-front costs and recurring costs for those consultants over the three-year horizon. Don't forget, even if you only intend to use them during the initial deployment, consultants have a way of returning year after year.

Any outside personnel who are not staff members of the company should be included under consultants. Now, consultants may have significant up-front costs in many cases and then recurring costs as they make adjustments, support your application, or expand the reach of whatever you're doing.

TRAINING

Finally, with many products, especially (but not, by any means, exclusively) software applications, there's often some user time spent on training. That airline, for example, will look closely at the cost of initial and recurring training for their pilots if they're purchasing an aircraft type that they don't normally fly. How many people will need training? How many hours will each person need to spend in training? Multiply the number of hours for each person by their fully loaded cost, then multiply again by the total number of people. Don't forget to include things like trainers' time and travel expenses.

OTHER COSTS

These are the five main categories of cost for any product, but there are others that will occasionally be an issue. Additional costs may include energy costs, disposal costs for old products, and so on. Be aware of these and include them in your calculation.

DEALING WITH DEPRECIATION

Depreciation is an accounting method that takes the cost of a product or service and spreads it out over the entirety of its "useful life." In other words, if a customer makes a big investment in a solution, they may pay everything up front, but if they're going to use that solution for five years, then the cost is spread out over those five years on the company's income statement.

When you make a large investment for a business, tax and accounting rules typically forbid you from writing it all off as an expense in one year. Instead, they require you to write off parts of it over the years of its useful life.

In general, I suggest *not* using depreciation as part of the ROI calculation when making a sales pitch, not if you want an accurate ROI calculation. Why? Because the money still comes out of the customer's pocket up front, and they're still making their buying decision based on that cost and its perceived value in the present.

Depreciation has more of a tax impact than an actual business impact. In a sense, depreciation means it won't cost the customer as much out of their income statement now, but it'll cost them a bit each year in future years. In other words, they can spread the costs out over future years, so while the money is coming out of their pocket right now, they can only tell the tax authorities about a small percentage of it now and then benefit from writing it off in future years.

However, when you're building a business case, adding depreciation makes the calculation needlessly complex. It also makes the calculation less accurate since the customer usually depreciates over a longer time horizon than your three-year ROI assessment.

Nevertheless, if you have to depreciate in a business case, include the depreciation charges in the year that they are incurred. For example, if a customer buys a piece of hardware for $100,000 but they have to depreciate that expense over five years, then the depreciation expense is going to be $20,000 a year for five years. However, your ROI assessment will only cover a three-year time frame, so you're only going to include the $20,000 depreciation expense from year one, year two, and year three.

Unfortunately, that means you're missing the costs for years four and five, which makes your projection less accurate and overly complex. That's why I recommend avoiding depreciation altogether in building your case.

Costs are an area in a business case where everyone can get agreement early on. Just remember to keep one-time and recurring costs separate. Go through each of the five categories of cost methodically, and it will become an easy process to get through. Just make sure you accurately assess the cost of personnel because that category can be a little tricky.

Assessing cost shouldn't be too difficult, but getting it wrong can derail the whole sale. One of the most common ways that I've seen people get it wrong is by adding too many costs or including costs that aren't actually there. For example, they might include interest charges, which are hard for a prospect to understand, or they might add opportunity costs, which are vague.

Again, to be clear, a cost is anytime money actually comes out of the customer's pocket. If money doesn't come out of their pocket, then it's not a cost to be included. Don't talk yourself out of a sale by making it needlessly expensive. Give the prospect a reasonable estimate of the cost that is easy to understand.

Once you've assessed the costs and presented them to the prospect, it's time to assess and present the benefits. This is where a lot of salespeople start feeling completely overwhelmed. Never fear! We're going to break it down as simply as possible.

TIP: AN EASY WAY TO INCREASE ROI

There's an easy way to increase the ROI in your sales pitch. Simply reduce some of the up-front costs in your calculation. Remember, the ROI calculation is the net benefit the product will give the customer divided by the initial cost. While you won't change the payback period by much, and while you should always strive for accuracy about the costs, you *can* nevertheless defer some of the cost in a way that increases ROI. The more you can reduce the up-front cost, the more you reduce the divisor to the ROI equation, thus increasing your ROI.

For example, if there are upgrades included with a software solution that would have been an additional charge, then those costs are ultimately baked into the lifetime of the product. Even though the cost is assured, it happens in a future year, so you can move those costs out of the initial year category to increase the ROI.

CHAPTER EIGHT

ASSESSING BENEFITS

It's scary, I know, but assessing benefits isn't as difficult as you think. If you categorize benefits correctly, you can prioritize them from strongest to weakest, and in so doing, you can strengthen your case. Bear in mind, a sales pitch is only as strong as the weakest benefit you connect to it, so don't be afraid to toss some benefits away! Only use strong benefits that a prospect will believe. Don't just pile a bunch of weak benefits onto the business case because you think "the more the merrier."

Two strong benefits are all you really need to make a compelling case! Three benefits are fine, but more than that can become a problem. And if you're presenting more than five benefits, then you're almost certainly making your case too complex for the customer to move forward with your solution.

Remember: focus on the strong benefits and discard the weak ones!

The ROI calculation is straightforward. Remember our equation:

$$ROI = \left\{ \frac{\overset{\text{YEAR}}{1} + \overset{\text{YEAR}}{2} + \overset{\text{YEAR}}{3}}{} \right\} \div 3$$

INITIAL COST

While just about anyone should be able to do this, there are some good tools online to help with the calculation. You can visit ROITool.com, where you can download a standard spreadsheet for free that will help you conduct these calculations.

You don't need a perfect ROI as much as you need a *credible* ROI. In fact, a lower ROI that the prospect believes is usually much better and more effective than a higher ROI that prospect doesn't believe. If you tell a prospect that your product will give them 25,000 percent ROI, not only are they unlikely to believe it, but you might just kill the deal. At the same time, if the ROI is too low, then the prospect will probably go with a competitor. Therefore, you need an ROI that is both believable *and* compelling!

The most *credible* ROI wins, not the highest ROI.

So let's look at which benefits are the most believable and the most compelling.

DIRECT AND INDIRECT BENEFITS

Salespeople and consultants often describe benefits as either *hard* or *soft*, but I want to change that to *direct* and *indirect*. In fact, talking about benefits as hard and soft only weakens some of them. No decision-maker likes the sound of a "soft" benefit, so it's not going to help your case.

In reality, any benefit is either directly or indirectly achieved by the customer, and that's how you need to communicate them.

How can you tell the difference between a direct and indirect benefit?

A *direct* benefit is something you can easily count, and it almost always involves a budget number. That includes things like cutting a budget number, saving some money, or a definite increase in profits. It's something the prospect can feel and touch.

An *indirect* benefit is anything you're not sure how to count, and it usually involves a gain in productivity in some way. In other words, it's something you *believe* will happen, but you can't necessarily put your finger on a specific budget number.

However, rather than benefits being binary (either direct or indirect), they tend to exist on a spectrum from *direct* to *indirect* and from *most believable* to *least believable*. We can order them from first order (the most direct and very believable benefits) to fourth order (the most indirect, least believable, and most variable benefits).

THE SPECTRUM OF BELIEVABILITY

Using four categories, you can quickly categorize benefits and understand whether they will be strong or weak. You can think of this as a graph with the horizontal line measuring a range from *direct* to *indirect,* and the vertical line measuring credibility from *believable* to *least believable.*

It looks something like this:

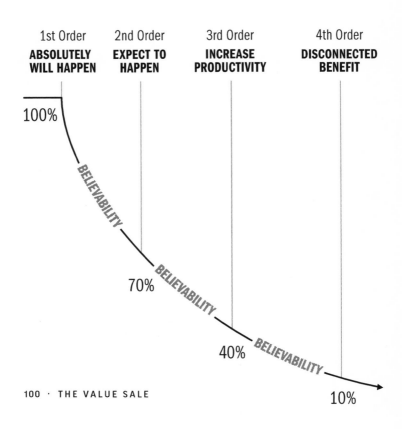

TYPES OF BENEFITS

Just remember, *presenting a benefit is more about credibility than anything else!* No matter how amazing the numbers are, the most compelling benefits are the ones that the prospect believes are true.

FIRST-ORDER BENEFITS

First-order benefits, otherwise known as "emphatic benefits," are things that will absolutely happen *and* are 100 percent believable. For example, let's suppose a company is trying to save money on manufacturing, and they have a chance to contract with an outside supplier. If they contract with the outside company to produce the product, they will be able to close one of their own underperforming factories, and that will save a large amount of money.

That's a benefit that is 100 percent believable and 100 percent likely to happen, which makes it a first-order, emphatic benefit. There is no question that if the prospect contracts with an outside company, the benefit will occur. They will absolutely be able to close the factory, reduce employees, and eliminate costs.

In a business case, a first-order benefit must be 100 percent believable by the prospect, and it must be clear that this benefit *will* happen. You can usually describe first-order benefits succinctly, and they include action verbs: we *will* reduce costs, we *will* cut service fees, we *will* redeploy staff, etc.

These are very believable benefits for the decision-maker, and the strongest benefits for your business case.

SECOND-ORDER BENEFITS

A second-order benefit is similar to a first-order benefit, but it always includes a "hedging" word. Its believability and likelihood are slightly less than 100 percent. What does "slightly less than 100 percent" look like?

When my daughter was a child, if she told me, "I *plan* on cleaning my room," it carried slightly less impact (and less than 100 percent certainty) than if she said, "I *am* cleaning my room." That's what a second-order benefit looks like. Basically, it means if the prospect takes a particular action, they believe it's *very likely* that they will experience the benefit. To use our earlier example, if a prospect contracts with an outside company, they think it's very likely that they will be able to close one of their underperforming factories (but it's not 100 percent guaranteed).

Using hedging words reduces believability, which makes second-order benefits less effective. Examples of hedging words include things like "we think," "we plan to," "we hope," "we'd like to," and so on. It's the difference between telling your boss you *will* do something or telling them you *intend* to do something. The impact is softened a bit. Second-order benefits are still very good, but they're not as strong or impactful as first-order benefits.

THIRD-ORDER BENEFITS

A third-order benefit is indirect, and its believability is generally around 50 percent. It's usually an increase in productivity, and rather than being a concrete number, it's more of an intuitive benefit.

Let's suppose you're selling an app for smartphones that is

going to make the prospect's job just a little easier. Is it going to increase their productivity? Certainly, but you can't necessarily put a concrete, believable number on it. It's a benefit that must be believed and accepted intuitively by the prospect.

Is it a third-order benefit? Only if the prospect *believes* they have a good chance of enjoying the benefit. If they don't, then you need to dump it and move on. On the other hand, if they *do* feel intuitively that this benefit is likely, then you need to determine how much more productive they think it will make them.

So if you're selling a smartphone app, you might ask the following question:

"Are you more productive in your job using a smartphone?"

"Yeah, sure."

See, the prospect agrees the first sentence is true. That's important. It can't be quantified; it's intuition.

"Do you believe you would be more productive if you used our mobile app?"

"I think so, yes."

"How much more productive do you *think* you would become?"

You're trying to figure out what the prospect believes intuitively about the third-order benefit, but that's the only way it's really going to work. Now, there's a good chance the prospect is going to answer this question with some version of "I don't know." At that point, you can provide a benchmark data point as a foundation for the question, but again, you're trying to get to *their intuition.*

"The average user becomes between 5 and 7 percent more productive at their job when using our mobile app. Knowing that, how much more productive do you think your employees will be using our solution?"

They'll probably offer their best guess.

Get them to the point where they believe the number is accurate and likely to give them a solid ROI from a sales perspective. It might not actually be the most accurate number, but that's not the point with third-order benefits. You're trying to come up with the highest number that the prospect will believe, and if it's a B2B sale, then it also has to be the highest number they can present internally.

If you need to get a more accurate number, I recommend conducting a survey of users, using current customer references, or running a small-site test of the product. Any of these are likely to get you a more accurate estimate about what the benefit is likely to be. You can also approach users of similar products or an earlier model, show them your product, and ask them what they think the increase in productivity *could be* using your product.

The least effective way of getting a number is to offer it to them. This is their business case, not yours.

Let's say they ask, "How much more productive will this smartphone app make our employees?" and you respond, "Oh, I'd say they'll be about 22 percent more productive."

That's not a good estimate. It's better to let the prospect come up with it themselves by asking a series of questions that moves them up the benchmark curve. Just remember, your goal isn't the number as much as it's the believability of the benefit!

When calculating a third-order benefit, be careful not to use the output but the *driver* to the benefit. Let's suppose a salesperson has a target of $1 million a year in sales, but that salesperson costs the company $100,000 a year "fully loaded." That means the company is spending $100,000 on this person to make $1 million. How much *more* would they be willing to spend on the salesperson if it would double their productivity to $2 million a year?

Rationally, the most they would want to spend to double their productivity would be the cost of hiring another salesperson, right? If they're spending $100,000 to make $1 million, then it makes sense to spend $200,000 to make $2 million. Now, that's not the value of the output; it's the value of the *driver* to the benefit, but that's the essence of a third-order benefit. You look at the people, not what the people are producing.

This is important because a financial decision-maker could always look at that third-order benefit and say, "Why buy your product to increase our productivity when we could just hire another employee? We would get the same value for the same cost."

Think about it. If I could double your sales, would you be willing to give me 50 percent of your sales? No, of course not. Then how much would you be willing to give me? The amount that it costs you to double sales, right? That's the real driver right there, the people who generate the sales, not the sales themselves.

A QUICK NOTE ABOUT BENCHMARKS

We'll talk more about benchmarks later. For now, just remember, benchmarks can be hazardous to your business case. After all, a benchmark is typically an average number, which means half the people will think it's too high, and half the people will think it's too low. Very few people will actually be on the line. So any benchmark data you use is likely to reduce the believability of your business case.

A better bet is to create a *range* around the benchmark number. For example, "We see the typical person getting between 3 and 5 percent. What do *you* think you will achieve?"

Mathematically, what you're doing is creating a range from a certain percentage below the average to a certain percentage above in order to encompass as many people as you believably can. Most prospects will then fall somewhere in that range, and when you ask, they will come up with a specific number that they feel comfortable with.

Remember, the goal here is credibility first. You can sacrifice a little accuracy. That doesn't mean you're trying to be inaccurate, just that you don't want to overstate what is possible and reduce credibility.

Let's use a concrete example. What if I had a piece of software that could reduce your inventory by 50 percent. How much would it be worth to you? Would it be worth the value of 50 percent of your inventory? Absolutely not! It would be worth the *carrying cost* of 50 percent of your inventory, or possibly the interest rate on it.

This is important because if a financial person in the prospective company does a review of the business case, they're not going to look at a product that can reduce inventory by 50 percent and say, "This is worth the value of 50 percent of our inventory." No, it's only going to be worth a tiny fraction of that amount. And then they're going to ask, "Could we spend that small amount on a better project to get a greater return?"

For that reason, when you're using third-order benefits, it's imperative that you focus on the thing that *drives* value for the customer (the people), not the value itself. Yes, this makes it an indirect benefit, but that's the point!

Third-order benefits have less believability and a lot of variability, but they are very important. Let's consider the example of Henry Ford. The biggest benefit he received in building the original Model T was in creating an assembly line, which dramatically increased the productivity of his employees. By increasing productivity, he was able to produce more, which reduced the overall unit cost. If someone had been pitching the assembly line to him, this would have been a third-order benefit, but it was the most important benefit he received. This is just one example of why third-order benefits shouldn't be overlooked.

Indeed, if you overlook productivity gains, then you might put yourself at a competitive disadvantage in pitching your product.

FOURTH-ORDER BENEFITS

Fourth-order benefits are typically comprised of long, disconnected stories, usually single examples where somebody got some benefit from the product. Sometimes, the logical flow of the story connecting the product to the benefit isn't all that clear. For example:

"I'm selling you an acorn. You can plant that acorn and grow a tree. You can use the wood from that tree to build a house. Isn't that wonderful? This acorn will create a house for you!"

There's a clear, logical disconnect between the action (planting an acorn) and the benefit (building a house). That's what makes it a fourth-order benefit. The distinction between a third-order and fourth-order benefit might seem subtle, so let's clarify. A third-order benefit may be indirect, but there's at least a clear connection between the action and the benefit. In the earlier example, the user holds the smartphone in their hand and the app makes them more productive, making it a third-order benefit. With a fourth-order benefit, this isn't the case. The action of planting an acorn only creates a house after multiple steps. That acorn could have just as easily resulted in a boat or firewood.

Let's suppose you're considering buying a customer relationship management system. Here's how a fourth-order benefit might sound: "This CRM system will make your sales reps more productive (a third-order benefit), which in turn will make them happier. Since they're happier, you're going to reduce employee turnover, which will reduce your HR costs. Therefore, this CRM system reduces HR costs (a fourth-order benefit)."

The salesperson will then tell the prospect a story about another customer who achieved reduced HR costs with the CRM system, but it's a disconnected benefit. There's not a clear connection between the action and the benefit. Rather, it's more of a by-product of the action that may or may not occur. Just because the sales rep can tell a story about a chain of events leading to the benefit for one customer doesn't mean it's likely to happen to others.

Unfortunately, many companies are very vocal about their fourth-order benefits. They make claims like "We changed the look of our store. That made customers happier, and because they were happier, they bought more stuff." It's *possible* that happened with *some* customers, but there's no clear, direct link between these two things.

Any estimate of the value of a fourth-order benefit is unlikely to be accurate, no matter how much effort you put into the calculation, and the wider the variation in an estimate from reality, the lower the believability of the benefit is going to be.

Should you *ever* include a fourth-order benefit in your business case? Personally, I think you should not. Just ignore them altogether. Typically, sales reps include a fourth-order benefit because it's a nice story about the product that they want to share. That story might be great for marketing material, but it just doesn't contribute to strengthening your sales pitch. You're better off not including it. Surely there are bigger benefits that the customer is going to achieve.

ORIENTING AND CALCULATING BENEFITS

Now that you have a framework for looking at benefits, think about all of the different benefits that the prospect is likely to achieve, and reorient them all from first order to fourth order. This will show you where to focus most of your energy. You want to give most of your attention to the first- and second-order benefits. What key studies, references, and solid estimates can you build around those first- and second-order benefits? How can you justify the numbers that you're giving for them?

One quick warning: looking for benchmark data to support your benefits is a pretty hazardous thing to do. Why? Because benchmark data is always old, and it's always based on surveys of some limited set of people that rarely correlates with the customer you're talking to (or, in many cases, reality). Just think about how many political projections have turned out to be wrong, and they're mostly based on surveys.

Also, there's really no such thing as average ROI. What if you walked into a shoe store, and instead of measuring your feet, the salesperson handed you an average-sized pair of shoes and said, "These are size eight, which is the average size and fits most people." Chances are, they wouldn't fit you. In fact, chances are they wouldn't fit most of the customers who walked through the door. Average shoe size doesn't tell you anything, and it's not helpful for buying shoes.

In fact, there's a lot of "average data" that appears interesting but is utterly useless for making a sale. Let's suppose the average commute for my employees from home to the company's main office is about forty-five minutes, but the average commute for the employees of the architectural firm in our building is thirty minutes. Would it make sense for me to take those averages and try to tell some prospective employee, "It takes, on average, forty-five minutes for employees to get to our office and thirty minutes to get to the architectural firm on the other floor. Therefore, it's better for you to become an architect?" That would be an absurd connection, but that's what people do with benchmark data. And it's useless.

If you're going to use benchmark data points, be cautious. It's better to use benchmark data as a *range* because then you're less likely to get pushback from the prospect. For example, it's better to say, "We typically see productivity gains of 3 to 5 percent," rather than to say, "This particular benchmark data point is 4.2 percent."

Remember, there are only three types of benefits, so let's look at each of them and discuss how you calculate an actual number that you can present to a prospect. Those three types of benefits are (1) **increased productivity**, (2) **reduced costs**, and (3) as a byproduct of the first two, **increased profit**.

Let's look at how you calculate them.

INCREASED PRODUCTIVITY

Increased productivity is usually realized as straightforward savings. To calculate an actual number, use the following equation:

number of people at fully loaded cost × *percent change in productivity* = *benefit*

To get the percent change in productivity, consider the following questions: How many people will use the solution? What's their fully loaded cost? What percentage of their time can they save with the new solution?

Note: always look at the percentage of *time* they can save, not how much more work they could do. And as we said earlier, don't look at the output of work, only the driver (e.g., not "They can generate 10 percent more sales" but "It's worth 10 percent of the fully loaded cost of a person."). You can use as many categories of productivity as you want: management productivity, employee productivity, etc.

REDUCED COSTS

When calculating reduced costs, answer the following question: what is the cost before, and by what percentage can you decrease or reduce it? For instance, companies that move to the cloud for their computing environment are able to reduce the cost of their internal IT departments and, in many cases, eliminate hardware that they've been paying maintenance costs on. Those maintenance costs that they no longer have to pay are a direct savings and reduced cost.

Let's go back to our airline example. That new aircraft may be 50 percent more fuel efficient than the aircraft they are currently using. Since fuel makes up a significant cost for all airlines, an increase in efficiency can result in a significant reduction in annual operating costs. That savings alone might justify the cost of purchasing new aircraft and the additional training for pilots.

INCREASED PROFIT

For this calculation, first determine the prospect's total annual sales. What's their profit margin, and what percentage can you increase it? Remember, it's not the increase in *revenue* but the actual increase in *profits*.

Increased profit is a somewhat dangerous benefit because there are a lot of things that impact profit, including market conditions. Often, it's not easy to tie the action that you've taken to an increase in profit. In some cases, though, it might be the only way to look at a change. For instance, buying that new combine might give the farmer more bushels of corn to sell, which would increase the farm's profit.

Generally speaking, you're still better off looking at productivity rather than the profit, but there are cases where it's impossible to do that.

LEAD WITH THE STRONGEST

As I've said, you can't just throw every benefit on a big pile and hope that at least some will appeal to the prospect. Including every benefit makes it more likely that you will derail your business case. Instead, present a few strong benefits, discard the weak ones, and focus your efforts on justifying the strong benefits as much as you can.

A few strong benefits are far more likely to close a deal and make it easier for your champion to make the business case internally to go forward with your solution. If you've ever had a deal that was received positively by your champion but stalled during the decision-making process, it was probably a weakness in the believability of your benefits.

You need to gather proof points that will bolster your claims and make your strongest benefits believable and compelling. How do you actually go about gathering those proof points? Let's find out.

CAUTION: KPIS ARE NOT ROI

Key performance indicators (KPIs) are management metrics used to measure the results of actions at an operational level. For example, a KPI might be the number of leads generated, the number of acres farmed, or the average transit time for a container ship. They provide insight into operations, but behind the scenes, management is converting these KPIs into cost or profit estimates. Reducing container ship transit time, for example, reduces fuel costs and might allow for more trips per year, increasing the profitability of the ship. Increased advertising, for example, would result in more leads, contributing to a larger sales pipeline and hopefully more sales. KPIs are very effective for setting objectives for teams, but are rarely monetary, so they can't be used when building an ROI business case.

CHAPTER NINE

GATHERING PROOF POINTS

Over the thousands of case studies I've conducted and sales situations I've been in, I've found that there are usually only one or two benefits that drive any deal, regardless of what you're selling, and two or three benefits that support it. There are *never* more than five. If you go over five, you've made a mistake. That means you can pour most of your energy into validating the two benefits that drive the deal by gathering *proof points*, because they are going to make the difference in building a compelling business case.

The best way to do this is to look at your **reference customers** that are similar to the prospect. In the case of B2C, that means an existing customer with similar demographics, interests, and needs who has already enjoyed some of the benefits you expect your prospect to receive. In B2B, that means another pharmaceutical company, another farm, another airline, or whatever other company is similar to the company that you're talking to that has experienced similar benefits.

If one company was able to increase productivity, and they have similar characteristics as the prospect, then it's likely that the prospect will experience a similar benefit. By now, you should already have an actual calculation *(number of people at fully loaded cost × percent change in productivity = benefit number)*. What you're doing at this point is validating that calculation, and the first way to do that is through reference customers.

Remember, it's not about accuracy but credibility. The most accurate number in the world does you no good if the prospect doesn't believe it. This is why, as I said, benchmark data is dangerous to use, because it's likely to show a number that's significantly higher or significantly lower than what the customer estimates.

Instead of using broad-based benchmark data, I recommend creating **your own database of benchmark data** based on your existing customers. Simply ask them what measurable benefits they've experienced from using your product. Not only will this give you a great database of ranges that you can apply to future customer estimates, but it will also help your customers understand the benefits you've delivered to them. I know of one company that conducts a benchmark survey during their annual user conference and gathers some great data with very little effort.

That, in turn, makes your current customers into stronger references that you can use in the future. You win in two ways. In simply surveying current customers, you develop stronger references by helping them understand the benefits you've delivered, and at the same time, you get the data you need to build a more compelling business case for future prospects.

A third way to gather proof points is a **pilot test**. You can pilot your product to a small set of users, then measure the outcome, whether it's increased productivity, reduced cost, or something else. By measuring the output, you can come up with a reasonably accurate number that a prospect is likely to experience after purchasing your solution.

The downside is that this delays the sale because it might take a month or two to conduct a reasonable estimate. After all, you have to estimate the baseline first, then determine the change to that baseline, and finally adjust for any variables (e.g., a change in the economy, reduction in demand, etc.) that may have occurred during that time. That's going to be time-consuming.

Fortunately, you don't always need to conduct the actual pilot test. Sometimes, simply showing the solution to a select group of users and asking them about it can give you valuable feedback. Simply ask them questions like "Would this help you? How much do you think it would help you? Where would it help?"

Finally, you can also develop proof points by turning to an **independent outside company** to build your business case. An internal value team might be useful for this, but for larger, more important deals, an independent assessment from someone who doesn't have any particular reason to give you a positive ROI might serve you well. Never use outside proof from a company with a vested interest in the deal, and never turn for proof points to the company or person who you plan to use for implementation.

Also, be wary of using proof points from certain large, popular consulting companies (who shall go unnamed). I've seen many business cases that were built on dubious foundations because they relied on proof points from large consulting companies who wanted to do an "impressive" job.

Remember, avoid broad-based benchmark data because it can apply to a wide number of companies. You're better off just surveying your customers and using their testimony as strong references about each of the benefits you've delivered.

VALIDATE EACH BENEFIT

For each of the strong benefits you've selected, make sure you gather enough data to validate them in the business case. It's a good idea to write a paragraph about how you've validated each benefit, using two or three different ways you've done it. For less important benefits, you can use just a single point of data to validate them. They're still important, but they're also likely to have higher variability.

Remember, you're using a range: "We estimate that the expected benefit could be from X percent to Y percent." Always use words like "expected" or "potentially" in communicating what the benefit might do for a customer, and considering including the worst-case scenario, such as "We think you're likely to achieve a 10 percent boost in productivity, but the worst-case scenario would be 7 percent." This shows the customer that even the smallest expected benefit is still good enough for them to make the investment and move forward. We'll look at generating a worst-case ROI in the next chapter.

A single ROI case study of an existing customer with a good number attached to it is almost always going to be stronger and more compelling as a proof point than anything else you can do, so connect it to your strongest benefit and your best marketing material.

Ultimately, your goal is to validate the benefits of your product, with a particular focus on the strongest benefits the prospect is likely to achieve. For each benefit, ask yourself: Do you have references or case studies that can support it? Do you have internal benchmark data or outside data that can support it? Keep in mind, external benchmark data is your weakest proof point but may be useful as a range.

What you *never* want to do is let salespeople come up with their own numbers. "I think this will reduce your cost by 10 percent." That always sounds weak. You need something to validate that number other than the salesperson's intuition or opinion.

If you're really stuck, then a pilot site is your best alternative to validate your proof points. However, a time-and-motion study (an analysis of the amount of time spent conducting various jobs) is rarely very accurate. Whatever you do, remember that credibility is the most important thing, not accuracy. You can break down your product or service into a bunch of individual steps, get a benefit estimate number for each of those steps, then add them all up and get a huge number. However, if that number is so big that a prospect doesn't find it believable, then you're not helping your case.

THE STRONGEST PROOF

To summarize, in a sales situation, your best options for gathering proof points (from strongest to weakest) are customer references (by a large margin); survey data from the prospect; benchmark data you've gathered from your own customers; data from an outside company that doesn't have an incentive to close the deal; a pilot site; and finally, benchmark data from an outside company. Generic benchmark data is almost always useless when generating a business case. Of those options, your most powerful validation comes from ROI case studies of your existing customers that are like your prospect—this proves the value of what you're doing better than anything else.

With these proof points, you can create a compelling case for your product, but even with the most compelling business case in the world, something can go wrong in the sales pitch. What do you do when the sale seems to be slipping away? Do you give up and walk away? Not at all. There's still a chance to get the prospect to move forward, and I'm going to show you how.

PROOF POINTS: FROM STRONGEST TO WEAKEST

1. customer references

2. survey data from the prospect

3. benchmark data you've gathered from your own customers

4. data from an outside company that doesn't have an incentive to close the deal

5. a pilot site

6. benchmark data from an outside company.

CHAPTER TEN

ADVANCED TECHNIQUES: WORST-CASE SCENARIO

What do you do when, despite your best efforts to get a prospect to move forward with you, something goes wrong and threatens to derail your sale? This can happen at any point in the process. Well, the good news is, no matter how or when it happens, you don't have to give up and walk away. There's still a chance to save the deal!

I'm going to give you a few advanced techniques to use when something goes wrong with your sale.

HOW TO IMPROVE THE BUSINESS CASE

Now, if you've done a breadth and repeatability assessment before the meeting, then you should already have an idea of how the sale is going to turn out. You should already have some sense of how strong or weak the ROI is going to be. Is there anything you can do to fix weak ROI? What if you're dealing with a skeptical prospect who is trying to be conservative in their expectations?

In that case, the best thing you can do is find a valid way to improve the benefit numbers or reduce the cost numbers so the customer feels better about the deal. The ROI doesn't have to be perfect. It just has to be strong enough and credible enough—not only against your competitors but against any other project that the prospect may be considering—to get the prospect to move forward with you.

PRESENT THE WORST-CASE SCENARIO

Since you're giving them the expected ROI, if you can show the worst-case ROI to still be positive, then you're going to assuage a lot of the prospect's hesitation. In a B2B situation, you need to make the prospect feel comfortable enough that they're willing to put their reputation on the line to argue persuasively that the project is still going to be positive even if they only get the worst-case ROI. What the worst case gives them is a floor. If everything goes wrong, what could happen? There's absolutely no sense presenting a best case. Nobody ever looks at it; nobody makes a decision on it. It just doesn't matter. Just present the expected case and the worst case.

Let's go back to that farmer purchasing the new combine. They might base their benefit on an expected 20 percent increase in yield but then satisfy themselves that they are making a good decision by looking at the worst case. If the worst case is only a 5 percent increase, but that's still good enough to justify the purchase, then they're going to feel comfortable that they are making a good decision.

If the worst case is still a positive ROI, then the prospect knows that even if things go wrong, they will still be in a good position. But how can you make a weak ROI number look stronger? Here are some tactics.

PRESENT MILESTONES

You can establish some milestones during deployment that the prospect will have to hit to ensure financial success. These don't necessarily have to be time-based. The prospect can achieve just about anything in any amount of time by simply hiring enough consultants to do it, but the price may be astronomical.

Milestones need to answer questions like the following:

- How quickly can they deploy the product?
- How quickly can they get their employees up to speed?
- How many employees do they need running the product within the first three or six months in order to start achieving a positive ROI?

This is where the worst-case scenario might come into play. What if they don't hit these milestones? For example, what if they can't deploy within some specific time period? What if they don't get enough users, or the users are fully trained but not interacting with the product? When will the new work truck arrive, and what happens if it's a few months late? Will they still be able to make money during the business's busy season? Do they need to rethink when they hire that new employee? How late can the delivery of the combine be for the farmer to still be able to use it during harvest season?

But what if the worst-case scenario reveals that if something goes wrong, the ROI could turn negative? In that case, they probably need to reconsider whether the risk is worth it or not, so the worst-case scenario might not help you. Now, no company relies only on worst case. If you ran your company on worst case, you wouldn't run a company. However, everything is a measured risk.

Of course, as I always point out to customers, if their employees don't use a product, then the ROI is always going to be negative, so user adoption is critical to any deployment. The farmer will never achieve ROI if neither the farmer nor the farmhands use the cutting-edge capabilities in that new combine, right?

The milestones identify what you expect to happen and what the ROI will be at each point, so you can identify the worst-case scenario and present what the ROI will be should the worst case happen.

ADJUST BREADTH AND REPEATABILITY

To improve the ROI for the worst-case scenario, take a look at *breadth and repeatability*. Is there some way you can increase one or the other in order to generate a better ROI? Can you increase the number of people who will use the solution, the number of times that it will be used, or both?

If an application is only going to be used a couple of times a year, is there a way you can present it so that it's being used more often? If it's only used by a few people, is there a way to show that it will touch more people? Find ways to connect the product to more people or an increased frequency, and you can improve the resulting ROI number.

REEXAMINE THE ROI CALCULATION

Next, you can look at the *ROI calculation* itself. Were you too conservative with your numbers? Did you underestimate the benefits that the prospect is likely to achieve? Being aggressively conservative will talk the prospect out of a likely purchase pretty fast. While you need an ROI that is credible enough to go forward, if you make it artificially low because you think it will be more credible, then you may be robbing your prospect of a great solution that could do them a lot of good.

Make sure your customer understands the real value being delivered. Don't talk them out of a solution by offering an overly conservative ROI number. Check again and make sure you haven't erred on the side of going too low. Maybe you've overestimated the costs. Are you charging too much up front? Take a careful look and see if you can boost that expected ROI number validly and believably.

I've seen many deployments where the up-front consulting costs hampered, or even killed, any chance that the application could deliver a positive ROI, so make sure you're not spending too much up front. If you can reduce those up-front costs, you will reduce the divisor in your equation and increase the resulting estimated ROI.

If you can't eliminate the costs, can you at least spread them out over future years? Maybe you can cut down on consulting costs to a point where you can get the deployment of your solution up and running faster. That way, the customer can start generating positive ROI sooner. Then perhaps they can do a second or third phase of the rollout with some of those costs rolled over.

The more you can cut up-front costs in your estimation, the greater the potential ROI you can present to the prospect.

TAKE A GOOD, HARD LOOK

Just because your initial ROI calculation isn't as strong as you need it to be in order to go forward, that doesn't mean all is lost. Take a good, hard look at the numbers and see if there's something you can do to make a more compelling case. There are usually a few different ways you can credibly increase the ROI estimation.

Once you've calculated the cost, calculated the benefits, and come up with a compelling ROI and payback period, it's time to deliver the business case. Now, you just need to tie it all together.

CHAPTER ELEVEN

HOW MARKETING DELIVERS VALUE

Before we tie everything together, we need to discuss marketing's role in all of this. We've looked primarily at how sales can use a value message to close more deals faster, but how can marketing deliver the same message? As it turns out, marketing's role is not that different from sales, and in fact, the two can work hand in hand to move prospects through the funnel.

Marketing, of course, creates the messaging and materials, but with a value approach, they're simply going to begin weaving value into everything they do beginning with lead generation. Value is like a spark that begins at the very first contact, which lights a fire that continues to burn brightly every step of the way.

That means early on, value has to be an integral part of the messaging, and it can't be gratuitous. It has to be real, although marketing has more latitude than sales in this regard. Marketing can rely a bit more on stories and doesn't have to talk constantly about ROI. They can still talk about benefits such as reduced cost and increased productivity, but they can also say that the product will make customers happier (something sales should avoid in the business case).

As with sales, the worst thing a marketer can do is to simply present a list of features and follow it up with the benefits. Instead, they need to lead with the benefits and then present the features that support them. Marketing is always, first and foremost, answering the question "What does the product do?" Don't answer that question with a bunch of features.

Instead, answer with how your company helps people (and potentially makes them happier) by reducing cost, increasing productivity, or increasing profit. Once you've done that, you can show how the features in your product support those benefits. Think about that plumber who is considering buying a new truck. What does he need that product for? To support a new employee. If he doesn't purchase the truck, that new employee won't be productive. So an effective marketing message would deliver value by showing how that new work truck could help him grow his business faster or complete more jobs in the same amount of time, ultimately making his plumbing business more profitable.

Forget the features-benefits list! That style of marketing went out years ago. Talk about the benefits first, and then talk about the group of features that drive those benefits. Do this with your new product, and do this with every upgrade of your existing products. Every time you make a revision to a product, give a compelling reason for customers to upgrade, beyond simply fixing bugs. How will the new version of the product help the customer to further increase productivity or reduce costs?

MARKETING AT EVERY STAGE

It's up to you to create a compelling message that will encourage prospects to move themselves through the funnel. Just like sales, your messages and content need to help prospects understand value in three stages:

1. **Stage one:** showing how your company delivers value in a broad-based way
2. **Stage two:** showing how other people like the prospect have achieved these benefits
3. **Stage three:** showing how the specific prospect will achieve these benefits

Reorient your marketing materials around these three stages of the value funnel, because your content is going to help sales move with the prospect through each of these stages.

All too often, I see marketers focusing chiefly, or exclusively, on opinions and top-level awareness, but what salespeople really need from marketing are proof points that will help them close deals. Instead of trying to make the funnel wider, as many marketers do, focus on increasing their win rate. Do that and you'll make your sales reps far more effective. They won't get frustrated so easily, they won't get overused and burned out, and they'll close more deals.

Too many lead-generation programs pull in leads without giving them a reason to be excited about the product because marketing is just trying to widen the funnel and pull in as many leads as possible. Look, it's incredibly expensive to make your salespeople process a huge number of leads. You're far better off making sure those leads already have an idea of the value they could achieve, and then those leads are more likely to become prospects who will walk themselves through the funnel.

MESSAGING FOR FUTURE PRODUCTS

It's important to assess your marketing material to make sure your benefits and features match. Are you combining multiple features together to support a benefit? Have you created a tight elevator pitch that could be boiled down to ten words or less? Are you clearly differentiating yourself from the competition? You wouldn't be in business if you didn't believe your product was better in some way, but are you better at increasing productivity or reducing cost over your competitor? If so, are you communicating that clearly in your messaging?

You begin doing this before your product even hits the market. Indeed, marketing should be working with product development to define the next product. If it's a battle between making something that's easy to use or making something highly functional, easy to use is always better. As the adage goes, "If the user can't use it, the ROI is always negative."

Never simply add functionality without taking into account the complexity of training customers to use it. Consider the state of aircraft technology today. Aircraft today, particularly small aircraft, are highly capable flying machines with sophisticated avionics that include a lot of automation technology. In fact, the typical cockpit is more user-friendly than ever before. No longer do you have the old-school round dials that were so prevalent twenty or thirty years ago. They've been replaced by flat-screen displays, moving maps, and plenty of information.

The way that information is presented to the pilot makes it very easy to use and consume, even in highly stressful situations. A lot of tasks that were hard work in the old days have become incredibly easy in newer airplanes, which has made long-distance flight far less taxing, even fairly routine, for pilots.

Consider the G1000 avionics system, which is popular in a lot of smaller aircraft these days. This sophisticated avionics suite provides a range of integrated systems that combine current weather data with a moving map using near real-time data. This replaces the need for all of the old charts and maps that pilots used to lug around. The same goes for a lot of things that used to be extremely difficult in the old days.

Let's suppose you're flying an airplane in the clouds during bad weather, and you need to find an airport. In the old days, this would have been a daunting prospect. Now, all you need to do is tap the NRST button and scroll through a list of the nearest airports. The G1000 will then draw a line from your plane to the chosen airport on the map display. Some systems will even dynamically calculate how far you can glide if your engine goes out, taking into account wind and terrain.

This is just one example of how product developers in the world of avionics technology have focused on creating user-friendly products, and when you do that in any industry, it becomes a lot easier to communicate the potential value to prospects. As a marketer, you can guide product development in this direction and use your messaging to present the value of upcoming products to prospects long before they even have that first meeting with sales.

In doing so, you set up the sales team for more success, and you encourage prospects to move themselves through the funnel at a much faster rate. You can then keep the momentum going by further focusing on value in your marketing materials at each stage of the funnel.

Ultimately, marketing should be best friends with sales. In many companies, and in many cases, they are not friends, and they're not really helping each other. Indeed, there's often a disconnect between what marketing creates and what sales needs in order to close deals. The best way to close a deal is through value, and marketing can help to deliver the value-based material that sales actually needs in order to get prospects over the line.

CHAPTER TWELVE

PUTTING IT ALL TOGETHER

Now it's time to develop your business case. Remember, your business case is going to contain as much text as it does calculations, so I don't recommend using automated tools to generate a full business case. If you decide to use an ROI tool, it should be used only for presenting calculations. There's no need to introduce additional complexity.

As you build your proposal, the business case needs to lay out the benefits that you expect the prospect to achieve and the justification for those benefits. Take into account the project costs, going through each of the categories of cost: *software, hardware, personnel, consulting,* and *training.* And orient benefits into first order, second order, third order, and fourth order, with particular emphasis on first- and second-order benefits. Remember, third- and fourth-order benefits are likely to have a much wider degree of variability and lower credibility.

When you're using a range of benefits, remember that your business case will be stronger the more you lean on measurable first- and second-order benefits because they are more believable to the prospect. Also, there will be less variability between projected ROI and achieved ROI. Conversely, the more you rely on third-order benefits, the weaker your business case will become, and the more likely you're going to need to use the worst-case scenario to get the prospect over the line.

Don't be afraid to throw away a second- or third-order benefit that has too much variation, especially if you have a strong first-order benefit with good ROI. And avoid using fourth-order benefits in the business case.

Once you've listed each benefit, justify them with survey data specific to your customer base, references from existing customers, references from similar customers in the industry, or pilot site data. Your ROI calculations don't need to use a complicated tool. You should be able to calculate them simply and quickly on a piece of paper using basic math. This is not complicated! Divide the expected benefit by the initial cost to get the ROI number.

Clarity, transparency, and credibility matter! The more straightforward you can make the calculation, the easier it's going to be for everyone to grasp it and understand what's happening.

Now is also the time when you want to calculate payback period. The easiest way to do that is to calculate how much the upfront costs are, how much the net benefit is per month, and how many months it's going to take to offset the initial cost. Remember, payback period is your strongest metric in a sales situation, and likely your prospect's strongest metric if they have to make an internal case to their company about why they should go forward with the project.

The final part of your business case should set out some milestones for achieving ROI, where you identify the targets the customer will need to hit to achieve the ROI that you've projected. When setting milestones to success, think about deployment and adoption first.

How many people will need to be deployed? When does the product need to be delivered? How much does the customer need to spend on consulting to make the ROI assessment? How many people need to be using the product within a certain time period to achieve the benefits. For example, maybe they need the entire team using the new application within the first three months in order to reduce inventory to the levels you expect by the end of the first year.

What do you do if your project is based entirely on third-order benefits because they give you a higher ROI, but the prospect is nervous about closing the deal because of it? One thing you can do is point out that the risk of the project may be worth the potential return on investment.

Now, if your product offers low potential ROI and a high degree of risk, then you're in trouble. But if you can show a high potential ROI, even with a high degree of risk, then there's still hope to close the deal. Take a look at some of the other projects the prospect has taken on. If most of them are low risk but low return, then you can say, "Hey, this is one project where you might want to gamble."

Most companies understand intuitively that they need to balance risky projects with less risky projects. They can't take too many risks, but they also can't be too conservative, or they're likely to be outmaneuvered. If they've invested in a lot of conservative projects, then they know they can take on a few risky projects. Sales can use this situation to encourage them to take a gamble on a riskier project, even if the pitch is weighted toward third- and fourth-order benefits.

THE ELEMENTS OF A COMPELLING BUSINESS CASE

To summarize, your business case will include the following:

- The benefits (lead with first and second order benefits)
- The projected costs in each of the five categories
- The actual payback and ROI calculations (remember, payback comes first, then ROI)
- The milestones to achieve success

And that's it. That's how you create a compelling case to sell a software application, a combine for farmers, a corporate jet, or whatever else you're trying to sell. You can include an appendix in your business case that contains all of the actual data you've referenced, but again, avoid automated tools that generate ROI based on a few calculations and benchmark data, unless you have a tool that is customized for your particular solution. A simple, free tool like ROITool.com, which is little more than an Excel spreadsheet, can be useful.

Over time, as the customers use your solution, check in with them to see how they're doing in achieving those milestones and make sure they're having a positive experience. What results are they achieving, and how can you help them continue moving forward? That will make them great references for future prospects.

TRANSPARENT AND CREDIBLE

Transparency and credibility are key to an effective business case. Build your case, make it easy to understand—a good business case is always relatively straightforward, not too difficult or complex—and focus on the most important benefits. Ultimately, it should be little more than stating the benefits, stating the proof points behind those benefits, and potentially stating the worst-case scenario for benefits that have a high degree of variability.

Don't make it any more complicated than that. You don't need to coerce them. You don't need to push them. You don't need to challenge them. Just show the prospect how you're going to deliver value, with clear and credible ROI, and you'll win more sales every time!

CONCLUSION

THE ART OF THE BUSINESS CASE

It comes down to one simple truth: if you prove value, a prospect will feel more comfortable going forward. Getting on a prospect's target list may be about marketing and visibility, but closing a deal is about proving that you're the best solution for them and that your solution will deliver the greatest value for the money they spend.

Building an effective business case to prove that value doesn't need to be difficult. All you have to do is understand simple concepts like the breadth and repeatability of your solution, the prospect's buying motive, and the benefits they're likely to achieve. Select the two or three benefits that matter most and focus on validating those benefits with credible proof points.

Your business case is only as strong as the weakest benefit, so including more than five is almost never necessary. While additional benefits might increase the ROI slightly, it's not going to be enough to change the decision process. Sales rarely hinge on one or two percentage points. Focus on just a few of the most compelling benefits, and you're more likely to build a business case that wins over your internal champion and the financial decision-maker within the organization.

VALUE WINS OUT

Look, there are a whole lot of sales techniques being promoted out there in the marketplace of ideas. Some will tell you to find the customer's pain point. Others tell you to challenge the customer in some way so you can keep them moving forward at each stage of the process.

You don't need any of these tactics. Just weave value into the sales funnel early on in the process, and you will ease the customer's transition all the way through the funnel. That's it. You don't have to push, pull, or force them through the sales funnel. Just use the carrot of value, and they will keep moving through the funnel of their own volition.

In fact, if a prospect sees the value you can deliver—the positive ROI for their investment—they will lead themselves through the funnel. That's it. You don't need any other sales techniques. You don't have to be locked in battle with a prospect, strong-arming them from stage to stage. Just show them value.

And the better you get at showing value at the beginning of a deal, the more effective you will become at getting a prospect over the line. That goes for both sales and marketing. Show value from the beginning, and you will shorten the time to close.

You will also reduce or eliminate pushback and the demand for discounts that are the bane of your existence.

Remember, if you're seeing deals stall out when they reach the next level of management or decision-making in a prospective company, there are ways to keep them moving forward. For example, you can use *payback period* to show the customer how much more money they're losing at each stage than if they'd already closed the deal.

THE CHANGING LANDSCAPE

The sales landscape has changed, thanks largely to the internet. These days, most prospects come to a deal with a relatively high level of understanding of your product. They probably already know your features and understand what your product does, so you don't need to waste a bunch of time educating them on the features.

Instead, show them how those features translate into benefits that they will experience. I recently bought a new car. Long before I ever talked to the sales rep, I had already done some online research about the car. I watched reviews on it and knew all of its features. There wasn't much that I needed the sales rep to teach me about the product, and if he'd spent time describing the plush leather seats, the sound system, the transmission, the telematics, and so on, he just would've been wasting my time.

By the time a prospect comes to you, they've already narrowed you down to a short list of potential solutions, and they're already self-educated on what your product does. It's your job to show how the product delivers value. How do all of those features deliver positive ROI? If you answer that question, and answer it well, you're going to win far more sales than with any other sales technique on the market.

So many of the salespeople I've worked with are afraid of using value in their sales pitch. It seems overly complex, and they're unsure how to connect value to a specific prospect. Hopefully, this book has made it a little easier for you. Communicating value is relatively straightforward, and you can calculate ROI with just a simple equation.

This goes for marketing as well. Value is not just for salespeople. In all of your marketing materials, don't make the mistake of just talking about the features of the product. Connect the features to specific benefits, show your target audience the value your product delivers at each stage, and they will be far more receptive to your message.

In sales and in marketing, value wins out every time!

ABOUT THE AUTHOR

IAN CAMPBELL is the Chief Executive Officer of Nucleus Research, where he is responsible for the company's investigative research approach, product set, and overall corporate direction. He is a recognized expert on the return on investment (ROI) and total cost of ownership (TCO) analysis of technology and has written and presented extensively on a range of organizational topics and the importance of matching technology to business organizational objectives. As an expert on technology value, he is a frequent speaker at industry and business events and has been quoted in major business publications, including the *New York Times*, the *Wall Street Journal*, and the *Economist*, and the *Financial Times*.

For over a decade, Mr. Campbell has taught a course at Babson College in Massachusetts on assessing the value of technology and is a frequent guest lecturer at Stanford University, the University of California at Berkeley, Massachusetts Institute of Technology, Harvard University, and Boston College.

In addition to his expertise in financial analysis, he is noted for his research identifying the human barriers to successful technology deployment and the strategies that can be employed to maximize user acceptance of new technology.

Prior to joining Nucleus Research, Mr. Campbell was the vice president at International Data Corporation, where he managed a portfolio of research programs in the US and Europe.

Mr. Campbell holds a Bachelor of Science degree in computer science and economics from Northeastern University and a master's degree in business administration from Babson College.

Made in the USA
Middletown, DE
05 January 2025